A Beginner's Guide to Aikido

A Beginner's Guide to Aikido

by

Larry Reynosa and Joseph Billingiere

JAB Enterprises
R & B Publishing Company
9085 Santa Margarita Road
Ventura, CA 93003
(805) 647-8783

Disclaimer

This book is presented only as a means of preserving a unique aspect of the heritage of the Japanese martial arts. The reader should consult a physician before engaging in any form of strenuous activity. To minimize the risk of training injury, nothing described or illustrated in this book should be undertaken without personal, expert instruction. The publisher and the authors are NOT RESPONSIBLE, in any manner whatsoever, for any injury which may occur by reading or following the instruction herein.

Second Edition, Third Printing, June 1993

Second Edition, Second Printing, December 1989

Second Edition, First Printing, March 1988

© J. Billingiere

JAB Enterprises
R & B Publishing Company
9085 Santa Margarita Road
Ventura, CA 93003
(805) 647-8783

Dedication

This book is rededicated to the true spirit of Aikido.

Acknowledgments

We would like to express our deep gratitude to all our teachers, fellow students, friends, and loved ones. Their advice, support and most of all, their patient understanding, has made it possible for us to realize the dream of this work.

The interview with Mr. Steven Seagal, and articles written by Mr. Mitsunari Kanai and Mr. Mitsugi Saotome have been reprinted in this book with the personal permission of each of these teachers. For that reason, we would like to express our special thanks to them. Special thanks also to Mr. Nobuo Iseri for his input and writing. We'd like to thank Mrs. Vicki Reynosa, Ms. Andrea Billingiere, Ms. Diane Allen and Ms. Michelle Jaeger for all their word processing help. Thanks also go to Mr. Matsuoka Haruo for the calligraphy drawings. Special thanks go to Mr. Paul Anacker for his editing, typesetting, publishing and computer expertise.

About the Authors

In creating this compilation of information for the beginning student, the authors were wary of its acceptance in the Aikido world. However, they are sure that a real need of help for beginning students exists. It is hoped that this book will, to some degree, satisfy that need. The authors offer this book in good faith and stand ready to accept whatever response they may get, in the same spirit!

Larry Reynosa began his training in Aikido in early 1974 under the teaching of Nobuo Iseri Sensei. In 1977, at a winter Aikido seminar, Larry was strongly influenced by the guest instructor, Shihan Mitsunari Kanai. During this seminar, he also met Francis Takahashi Sensei and Pablo Vasquez Sensei, instructors from the Los Angeles area, both of whom were also to have a major influence on his Aikido career. Larry eventually received his first black belt under the guidance of Takahashi Sensei.

Since that time, Larry has himself served as chief instructor of three dojos; ranging from space in a local community center, to a full-time professional dojo, and most recently to a beautiful Japanese-style dojo built in his backyard.

In 1983, Larry was impressed by Shihan Steven Seagal, who recently returned to the United States from many years of study in Japan. This new influence motivated Larry to re-dedicate himself as a student after years of being "a teacher." He began to travel on a regular basis to the Tenshin dojo in Hollywood, California, to study under Seagal Sensei. Currently, he maintains a commitment to both that dojo and his own Makoto dojo in Ventura, California.

Joseph Billingiere began his Aikido training under Larry Raynosa in 1983. Together, they traveled to study under Seagal Sensei. As student and teacher, and also as friends, the authors use much of their travel time (and perhaps too much of their social time), to reflect on the changes that Aikido training had brought in their lives and in the world around them. Those reflections eventually grew into this book.

Joseph Billingiere holds a Ph.D. in Management Science and works as a Human Relations Management and Computer Consultant in the Ventura and Santa Barbara, California area.

Table of Contents

Dedication v

Acknowledgements vii

About the Authors ix

List of Calligraphy Figures xii

Chapter 1   Introduction 1

Chapter 2   Aikido is for Everyone! 5

Chapter 3   About the Founder 9

Chapter 4   Japanese Language and Culture 15

Chapter 5   The Dojo 19

Chapter 6   Dojo Etiquette 27

Chapter 7   Attire and Weapons 31

Chapter 8   Mat Survival 41

Chapter 9   Ranking and Promotional Exams 51

Chapter 10   Aikido in Perspective 65

Appendix A   Shihan Steven Seagal 71

Appendix B   Shihan Mitsunari Kanai 95

Appendix C   Shihan Mitsugi Saotome 103

Appendix D   Exercises 107

Appendix E   Vocabulary and Terminology 113

List of Calligraphy figures

Makoto v

Irimi 1

Deshi1 5

Sensei 9

Kokyu 15

Dojo 19

Maai 27

Shinken shobu 31

Ukemi 41

Kamae 51

Tenkan 65

Mushin 71

Shugyo 95

Takemusu Aiki 103

Tai sabaki 107

Montei 113

All of the terms are explained in either the vocabulary list in Appendix E or the text.

.

CHAPTER 1

Introduction

A *Beginner's Guide to Aikido* is a heartfelt effort to provide answers to the many questions both asked and unasked, that are common to the beginning Aikido student.

The early days of Aikido training can be an overwhelming experience for the body, mind and spirit, full of excitement and confusion. At a time when it seems that all of your attention must be focused on the physical aspects of Aikido, you find yourself surrounded by strange customs, language and even stranger discussions! "What are they talking about?" "Who's that?" "A what?" "Should I ask?" "Can I ask?" These are some questions common to beginners. Other questions are, "How can I learn more about this?" "What should I do in between training sessions?" "Isn't there a book available that I can take home?"

After years of observing the unnecessary confusion resulting from these unanswered questions, of seeing good people leave Aikido in frustration before ever really giving themselves a chance, the authors decided to do something about this problem. This book is the result.

There are many excellent books on Aikido available. Most of these are written by acknowledged Masters of Aikido and either interpret the philosophy of Aikido or provide precise step-by-step teachings of specific techniques. *A Beginner's Guide to Aikido* is both different and unique. This is a book written by students for the benefit of their fellow students and offered in the spirit of advice from a caring older sibling.

This is a book about how best to approach the study of Aikido and how to adapt yourself to a new and exciting world. You will find some basic do's and don'ts for the beginner and an introduction into the rich cultural, ritual, and social environment which is an integral part of the true study of Aikido. While there is no substitute for consistent training, this book can provide a continuity of the learning experience between training sessions and allow the student to come to the dojo with greater feelings of self-confidence and belonging.

A Beginner's Guide to Aikido consists of original writings of the authors, collected articles on important topics written by recognized Masters of Aikido, and other resource material which will serve as valuable reference guides now and for years to come.

The material in this book should be read, re-read, and then read again. Aikido is an "open ended system." This means that new levels of understanding continuously unfold throughout your years of training. You come to Aikido with some basic preconceived concepts; then, as you begin your training and the expansiveness of the Art opens up to you, your training gives you new concepts to consider, new physical skills to develop, and new arenas in which to evaluate yourself. Each re-reading of the important information in this book will bring a deeper understanding and a greater appreciation of Aikido.

To all our fellow students . . . ONEGAISIMASU!*

*Here is your first opportunity to use the Common Dojo Phrases section of Appendix E in this book.

CHAPTER 2

Aikido is for Everyone!

Aikido can be studied by people of either gender and of any age. Aikido students include philosophers, doctors, lawyers, oilfield roustabouts, secretaries, nurses, police officers, housewives, and grade school students. The motivation behind each individual's study of Aikido varies from the desire for a good form of exercise, to a desire to study a traditional Martial Art.

The study of Aikido is a cooperative rather than a competitive process and provides the opportunity to participate in a contact activity in a very active, but non-violent manner. It gives us the opportunity to work at our own pace depending on our age and our desires. Aikido training is one of the more aerobic martial arts. Each student maintains control of his or her individual workout level. Individuals interested in the benefits of gentle stretching can easily practice side-by-side with the most vigorous student. Whatever the desire, Aikido is not a spectator activity. Learning comes through doing and through relating to others on the mat. Finding individuals who have the same goals is not difficult, but you must be on the mat in order to do so. You must work with many different students because they will continually provide different stimuli for different kinds of practice. During this learning process, you must always strive to keep an open mind. By doing this, your technique will become more diverse and take on more meaning.

One of the hardest things to overcome for beginning students is the feeling that you are not good enough to work out in a particular class that is being taught; an advanced class for example. This is wrong! Aikido is the most humbling of all experiences. It requires us to put aside much of what we have learned in life and open ourselves to new and better ways. We must re-learn our most basic skills of breathing, moving, and seeing. Nothing could be more difficult, more challenging, or more rewarding. How silly it would be to think that we could go into a dojo and already know more about something that somebody else has been practicing for years, simply because we're older or perhaps more intellectual or physically strong. Learning something that has great quality can never come quickly. Just as a finely crafted piece of art takes time to create, the learning of Aikido requires years of study. We must develop patience with ourselves and then add to that by learning patience and understanding of others.

The following is an excerpt from a small article written by Mr. Nobuo Iseri Sensei. "Aikido can be an important factor in the developmental sequence of growth and maturity within ourselves, because it stimulates adaptive perceptual motor responses to help us more effectively cope with our environment.

Aikido stimulates basic awareness of the senses of touch, gravity, balance, body position, body pressure, sight, sound, smell, heat, energy, time, space, and intent. In a survival context, Aikido is an activity of learning to develop immediate and appropriate responses to threatening situations in order to maintain personal safety and equilibrium. Complex physical situational responses must normally be dealt with on a thinking level and worked out methodically. The goal in Aikido is to attain automatic reaction for protection of the self.

"The non-competitive nature of Aikido training adds a dimension of mutual trust and protection. This attitude of trusting care becomes an integral part of the developmental process of one's interaction with his or her environment.

"As the individual matures, the cognitive function comes to dominate, thereby giving rise to a defense system separate from the body. The development of body knowledge may come to be retarded or misguided, leading to further separation of mind and body. Without an integrated defense system, the individual is open to feelings of anxiety and insecurity. Aikido training will help the individual to integrate the psychological and physical defense systems."

*Nobuo Iseri is the Chief Instructor at the Moving Center Dojo in Ventura, California. Iseri Sensei is a 5th degree black belt, who has practiced and contributed to Aikido for over 30 years.

CHAPTER 3

About the Founder

Morihei Ueshiba

To the new student of Aikido, Morihei Ueshiba, more fondly referred to as O'Sensei, often seems to be a very mysterious, even mystical, figure. The senior members of any dojo speak of him in deferential terms and obviously hold him in great respect, if not awe. "Who was this man?", "What makes him so great?", and "Why should I, as a student of this Art called Aikido, respect him?" Even when students ask these questions, the answers are usually vague, confusing and not satisfying. However, human nature soon takes over and in response to peer pressure and a normal need to be accepted by their new group of friends, students quickly adapt and conform to the outward signs of respect and acceptance of O'Sensei, which is the group norm. This is Phase one.

In Phase two, the student develops an appreciation of the incredible beauty, logic, and power in the movements and techniques of Aikido. In addition, many students become aware of the positive effects that Aikido has on other, seemingly unrelated, areas of their lives. At this point the student begins to realize the enormous potential of Aikido and the kind of genius it took to create it. Along with this new understanding comes a new, enhanced sense of respect and curiousity concerning O'Sensei.

As students of Aikido, we have all chosen to follow the "Way of Ueshiba", and we should therefore strive, in all ways, for a greater understanding of Ueshiba, the Man; his personality; his strengths; and the circumstances and events which helped to shape his life and led eventually to his creation of Aikido.

Like all great men, Morihei Ueshiba (1883-1969) was a man of seeming paradox. He was a man of true "Budo", a modern samurai, who exemplified the martial heritage of his culture. He was a man of strong emotion, dedication, and dynamic personal power and at the same time he was a man fully committed to his pacifist religious philosophy.

Aikido is the blending of these diverse elements of his personality, into a form that we may all use to make our lives better. Aikido is his legacy to the world.

The following is a brief sketch of some of the important people and events in the life of O'Sensei. It should be considered only a starting point for your own research and investigation into this truly remarkable man:

December 14, 1883 .... Founder born in Wakayama Prefecture now known as Tanabe.

Early teens .... First formal study of Jujutsu at the Kitoryu dojo and Swordsmanship at the Shinkage-ryu Training Center.

1903 .... After two tries, became infantryman in the army during the Russo-Japanese War.

1912 .... At age 29, moved to Hokkaido and the village of Shirataki. Here he met the grandmaster of "Daito-ryu Aiki Jutsu" Sokaku Takeda.

1917 .... On his way to be with his dying father, met the master of Omoto-kyo religion, Inisaburo Deguchi.

1925 .... Many encounters with spiritual world that led to his belief that "The true purpose of Budo is love, the love that nourishes all beings." Age 42 years old.

1927 .... Onisaburo Deguchi encouraged Ueshiba to separate from the Omoto kyo and begin his own "Way". He did so and moved to Tokyo.

1931 .... "Kobukan" (Present day Hombu dojo) finished.

1932 .... Japan "Budo Enhancement Society" founded with Ueshiba as Chief Instructor.

1942	Left the Kobukan to his only son Kisshomaru Ueshiba and returned to the farmlands of Ibaraki Prefecture and the village of Iwama. Also, the year the name "Aikido" first used.
1942-1952	O'Sensei seemed to consolidate techniques and perfect the religious philosophy of Aikido.
April 26, 1969	At age 86, O'Sensei passed away.

Doshu Kisshomaru Ueshiba

Kisshomaru Ueshiba is the son of the founder of Aikido, Morihei Ueshiba. He was born in June 1921 at Ayabe in Kyote Prefecture. Much like his father, during his childhood Doshu spent a great deal of his time reading. In September of 1946, he received a degree in Political Science from Waseda University. During his school days, he trained directly under the Founder. He also studied swordsmanship at the Katori School and Kashimi School with his father.

In 1948, he replaced his father as the administrative head of the Aikikai Foundation's Hombu Dojo after the Founder had grown tired of the city life and moved to Obaraki Prefecture and the village of Iwama. Then, in 1956, Kisshomaru was installed as the director of the Aikikai Foundation.

During the years that followed, Kisshomaru Ueshiba was to become well-known for his Aikido ability. He was invited by instructors in Hawaii and the United States mainland to visit their dojos, which he did in 1963. His stay involved teaching and providing demonstrations in many dojos. In 1966, he was awarded the title of Earl by the Archbishop of Brazil in recognition of meritorious work in spreading Aikido. The following year he was appointed Chairman of the Board of the Aikikai Foundation on the occasion of construction of the new Hombu Dojo.

Kisshomaru assumed the title of Aikido Doshu in May of 1969 after the death of the Founder Morihei Ueshiba. Since taking on this tremendous responsibility, he has maintained and developed the art that his father had established.

Doshu has also been appointed Director of the Nippon Budokan Federation. He had made several trips to the United States in the last few years and continues to be an inspiration to many of us that have come to know him, not for being a copy of his father, but for the great man he has become in and of himself.

Doshu has contributed much to the literature of Aikido, having written many articles and books about Aikido.

CHAPTER 4

Japanese Language and Culture

Importance to Learning Aikido

*A*s Aikidoka (students of Aikido), we seek an understanding of the Japanese language and culture. We do this for the same reason we might read the writings of a famous author in the author's native language—to get as close as we can to the original meaning of the author for better understanding. This does not mean we should have a goal of becoming Japanese-like. This would not necessarily enhance our study of Aikido. If, however, we find aspects of the Japanese culture to be beautiful and desirable, we should feel free to enjoy them as one more beneficial aspect of our study.

Becoming familiar with a different culture is an exciting and rewarding adventure when it is approached with an open and accepting mind. A different language, different foods, different clothes, different customs, and often even a different perception of reality are all part of this experience. However, it is not the differences, but the similarities which are most enlightening. For example, if we begin to think of the well-known Japanese custom of bowing as something akin to the western custom of handshaking, we can then appreciate both actions as merely different manifestations of the same basic human need. This analogy may not be perfect, but it can help us begin to remove some of the mystery often associated with the study of Aikido.

In many dojos that have Japanese senseis (teachers), the Japanese language and customs are more strictly followed. In dojos that have non-Japanese senseis, these customs are often set aside. As a student in any dojo, one must be careful to accept the way each sensei has chosen to teach Aikido in that dojo.

Whether or not the Japanese language and customs are stressed, there will always be basic protocol practices. (For a discussion of protocol and its importance to you, the beginning student, please refer to Appendices A and B). Don't be surprised, when you visit another dojo, that they do not open, conduct, and close classes the same way *your* sensei does. Respect everything when you visit a dojo and experience the Aikido that is there.

It is the opinion of the authors that the Japanese language and customs are important and conducive to the learning of Aikido. If you can understand and use the language used in Japanese dojos, you can usually practice Aikido anywhere and feel comfortable. If you don't make the effort to learn the terminology, you will be forced to translate first, then train, thus losing valuable mat time. Also, someone who has attained the rank of yudansha (black belt) may find it somewhat embarrassing to practice at a more traditional dojo and not be able to understand the terminology. A student of Aikido should be a student of all the aspects of Aikido training. One should make an effort to find out as much about Aikido as possible whether or not your sensei stresses those aspects. In Appendix E, you will find a list of basic vocabulary and terms used in Aikido dojos. This list is by no means all-inclusive, but it will provide you with an understanding of many commonly used words and phrases.

CHAPTER 5

The Dojo
Where Your Training Begins

The word *dojo* literally means "place of the way." The dojo is a place of learning. It is a place to respect, to keep clean and to care for. A dojo is a place to be made special for the practice of a special Art.

Aikidoka can and will train anywhere and everywhere; backyards, garages, youth centers, basements, warehouses, etc. It is important to remember that the place where Aikido is practiced becomes, at least symbolically, a dojo and must be treated as such. All students should take the responsibility to help whenever they can to keep the dojo clean, and to contribute actively to the maintenance of the dojo. This is part of the reality and the tradition of Aikido. Consider it a part of your training. Eventually you will come to appreciate its inner value. Each beginning and advanced student should actively seek to be the first to the brooms and wash rags, before and after practice.

Advanced students should actively strive to be role models for newer students.

In the following discussion, please refer to the diagram showing a basic dojo. Again, we remind you that your dojo may vary from this illustration, so it should be viewed as only one way a dojo could be set up. However, the diagram will call attention to the important parts of any dojo and give basic rules for addressing these parts. When entering the dojo through the main entrance, (1) one should perform a formal standing bow (ritsurei) towards the Kamiza (7). The student should then proceed immediately to either the public seating area (2) if not practicing, or to the shoe rack (3) where shoes are removed and stored until the end of class. Typically, the sign-in sheet is next to the shoe rack so each student can keep record of practice hours. Each student should make sure to sign in, as the sensei will not do it for you. If students have brought their own personal weapons, they should either place them next to the weapons rack (4) or on the rack itself. If there are weapons in the rack already, make sure that your weapons are clearly marked so you can identify them easily. (It can be very embarrassing for others, if they assume your weapon is a dojo weapon, start to practice with it and you have to ask for it). As you step on the mat (17) to go to the dressing area, you should again perform a standing bow towards the Kamiza and picture of O'Sensei. Students should then proceed down the left wall (in this dojo, this side of the mat would be called the shimoseki (9) (lower seat) where the nafudakake (5) (name board) is typically hung. The nafudakake should have all members listed in order of rank. (Note: The sensei of the dojo or a designee should be the only ones to touch or reorder the names on the nafudakake).

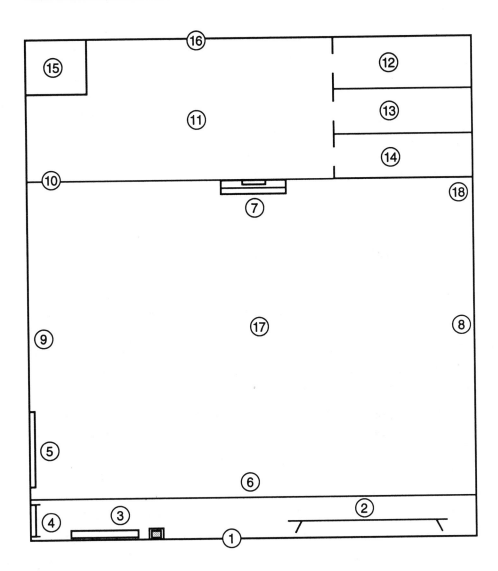

1. Main entrance; 2. General public seating; 3. Student shoe rack & sign in;
4. Weapons rack; 5. Nafudakake; 6. Shimoza; 7. Kamiza; 8. Joseki; 9.
Shimoseki; 10. Mat entrance; 11. Lounge area; 12. Men's dressing room;
13. Women's dressing room; 14. Office; 15. Bathroom; 16. Rear entrance;
17. Mat area; 18. Starting position for sweeping.

Students should not waste a lot of time getting dressed because there will always be other things to be done before class begins. Students should use the dressing areas (12) and (13) to store their clothes and gi bags. If you find that new students have come in to join the dojo, you should make an effort to make them feel comfortable and show them around. An important thing for regular members to show beginning students is the correct way to wear their gi and how to mark them so they will not be misplaced. (Note: Regular members should take this responsibility and not leave it solely up to the sensei).

Once you are dressed, you should look for things to do to help maintain the dojo. Most important is to get a broom and help sweep the mats down (refer to diagram of sweeping the mats). Other students should be dusting any shelves, pictures, furniture, etc. Make sure all brooms and dust rags are cleaned and then placed back into the storage closet and out of the way. (Note: If everyone takes responsibility for helping, the task of cleaning will take only a few minutes).

Now you are ready for practice. Upon entering and leaving the mat area through the dojo entrance (10), one should always perform ritsurei towards the Kamiza. Remember, if you as a regular student do not adhere to dojo etiquette, the beginners that are watching (and believe us when we say they are watching) will not adhere either. Please accept this responsibility out of respect for the Kamiza and O'Sensei.

Approximately five minutes before the class is scheduled to start, take a seat (depending on your rank) at the lower seat (6) and sit quietly facing the Kamiza. This is time for quiet meditation. Your sensei or dojo sempai will start class on time, so make sure you are ready on time.

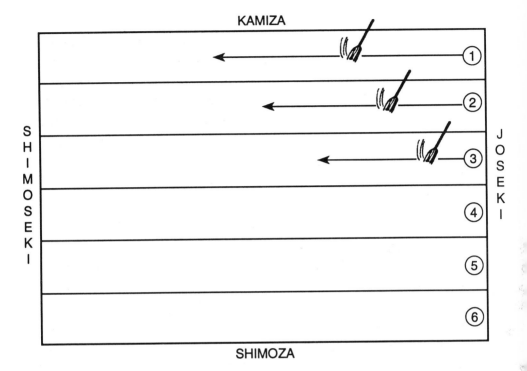

Sweeping the Mat

The mat can be swept very quickly and efficiently in the manner shown. The number of brooms may vary; three are shown for example. Students take positions 1 to 3. The first student sweeps out the corner and feeds the dust to the second student. The first then proceeds across the mat from joseki to shimoseki, constantly feeding the second who in turn feeds the third. When the first reaches the other side, he starts again at position 4. The second goes to 5, etc., until the entire mat is swept. When restarting, the students do not cross the unswept part of the mat.

At the time class is to start, all students should form very neat rows across the mat at the shimoza (6). If you find new students still wandering around, please make sure they follow suit in sitting in seiza with the rest of the students.

As your sensei or sempai starts towards the Kamiza to begin class, remain still and quiet with your back straight and look straight ahead. Your sensei or sempai will be seated in front of the Kamiza and perform a formal sitting bow (zarei) towards the Aiki Shrine (if there is one) and the picture of O'Sensei. This you should also perform with your sensei. Your sensei will then turn to face you and again perform a formal bow to you and the rest of the student body. At this point the sensei will start the class by either doing taiso or go right into technique training. (Note: This is a good point to let you know a little about the opening bow ceremony just described. When a shrine is present, a formal bow may be performed towards the shrine before a formal bow is performed towards the picture of O'Sensei. You might wonder why anything in the dojo would come before O'Sensei, but remember that before O'Sensei's death, he too, opened the class in the same manner. So, the Aiki Shrine was shown respect by O'Sensei before class also. Another important aspect of the formal opening bow is the hand clapping. This too will vary from dojo to dojo depending on the background of your sensei. It is said that the claps of the hands send out a vibration into the spirit world and call attention to the spirit of O'Sensei. The vibration then returns to the dojo in the form of an echo and the air is thick with "Ki". The number of claps and number of bows will vary, one to four. (Please refer to the interview with Seagal Sensei in Appendix A for more information on meaning of hand claps).

A formal opening bow should be performed alone, for example if you come in late. If this should happen, make a formal sitting bow immediately after stepping onto the mat, then sit in seiza until your sensei or sempai invites you to join the class. At that time join in with whatever is taking place on the mat.

(Additional note on coming to class late: It is your responsibility to join class as quietly and unnoticeably as possible. Make sure you know how your sensei wishes you to enter class late).

As you will find out, all opening ceremonies are not the same. The most important aspect of this ceremony is that whatever is the custom of your dojo or a dojo that you may be visiting, make sure that you follow it out of courtesy and respect for the dojo and sensei with whom you are about to practice. Do not be so narrow-minded as to be offended by any variation in the opening bows.

When the class is finished, all students should quickly take a seat at the shimoza and wait for the closing bow by the sensei. After the sensei completes the bowing ceremony, *do not* get up immediately. Stay seated and allow the sensei to leave the mat or verbally excuse everyone. Once the sensei is off the mat, students should bow to each other, or at least to the people with whom they practiced during the class, thanking them for their time and effort. The mats should then be swept down and wiped with freshly rinsed rags. *All students should take this responsibility!* It can be very embarrassing to see some students ready to sweep and clean only to have to wait for some students who have decided that they need a little more work on some technique shown in class! This is not only discourteous, but selfish. If you need to work on some of the techniques shown in class, you can do so after the mats are swept and cleaned. You should always try to help in some way if you can, but if you must leave in a hurry, you should feel free to do so. Then, after the next class, you should try to stay a little longer and do a little more to make up.

CHAPTER 6

Dojo Etiquette

Rules of Behavior

The subject of etiquette and its importance to the study of Aikido is a recurring theme throughout this book. In this section we have provided an overview of the etiquette related behaviors practiced in the Aikido Dojo. If a student is familiar with these behaviors he or she will be able to move comfortably through any Aikido class despite the small stylistic differences found from dojo to dojo. The following guidelines are important:

- A standing bow should be executed when entering and leaving the Dojo and also when entering and leaving the mat area of the Dojo.

- *Mokuso* is a call to attention by the Sempei or the Sensei. When you hear this (usually said in a rather loud manner) you should make yourself ready to practice. This is also used as somewhat of a command for you to go into a meditative state of mind.

- The formal bow at the beginning and end of practice consists of one or two seated bows toward the shomen (front wall of the dojo where O'Sensei's picture is), and then a mutual bow between teacher and students. The form and complexity of this ceremony marking the beginning and end of class varies somewhat from place to place, so in the case of a visiting instructor, his or her example should be followed.

- Effort should be made to be on time for class, but if unavoidably late, a student should perform the formal bow individually before beginning to practice. If it is necessary to leave class early, a student should inform the instructor and do an individual formal bow at the close of his or her own practice. In this case a formal bow consists of a sitting bow (zarei) towards the kamiza. A single bow is sufficient. Don't disturb the rest of the class.

- Onegaisimasu ("please", or "I ask a favor") and Arigato gozaimasita ("thank you") are the expressions used at the beginning and end of class, respectively, and also between partners at the beginning and end of class, respectively.

- Traditionally the instructor is addressed as "Sensei" in the dojo. However, the extent to which this custom is followed depends on the individual instructor. (Please see interview with Seagal Sensei for further discussion of this, Appendix A)

- The proper way to sit during class is in seiza—the formal Japanese sitting posture. A cross-legged sitting position is acceptable is seiza is impossible. If a student has a particular problem with knees or feet that interferes with the ability to sit in seiza, make sure the instructor is informed of the problem. In any case, an attentive posture should be maintained. Slouching, slumping, or leaning is not conducive to the practice of balance and centering! Students should not sit with legs outstretched.

• Students should not sit with their backs toward the shomen (wall with picture of O'Sensei); traditionally this is the place for the instructor or master to sit while watching class. If it is necessary to pass by when people are lined up in seiza facing the shomen, walk in back of them rather than in front.

• After the instructor demonstrates a technique, students bow, choose a partner quickly, and begin to practice. When the end of a particular practice is signaled (often with two claps), students should stop practice immediately, bow to their partners, and quickly line up in seiza for further instruction.

• For reasons of safety, respect, and courtesy, it is essential that the teacher's instructions be followed exactly. Many Aikido techniques can be dangerous if not practiced properly. Emphasis should be placed on learning as much as possible through intent observation and concentrated practice. Questions should only be asked when really necessary.

• Gis should be kept clean, and fingernails and toenails should be kept short. No jewelry should be worn during practice. Do not use alcohol or drugs before class.

• The mat should be swept before and after each class. Many dojos will wipe the mats down with freshly rinsed rags in addition to sweeping. It is the students' responsibility to keep the dojo clean. Dojo literally means "place of the way." It should be a place for misogi (purification) and for our sincere personal work.

Observation of these forms of etiquette will help to create a good atmosphere in the dojo. But more important than the superficial observation of any form is the sincere and open-hearted attitude toward training which gives meaning to the forms.

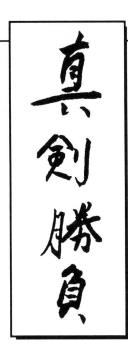

CHAPTER 7

Attire and Weapons
Care and Use

*T*he *dogi,* or *gi,* as it is known in casual terms, is the three-piece uniform that students should wear during practice. Typically, in Aikido you will find the single-weave, all-cotton gi to be most popular and the most durable. The fabric and weight of the gi is not very important for the beginner, although as you continue to practice, you will acquire a liking for one kind or another and this choice is really up to you. Regardless of the weight, make, or style of gi, they are all cared for in the same manner.

When donning the gi, first put on the pants. Make sure the little loop goes right under the belly button. Pull the draw strings tight and then thread the strings through the little loop in the opposite directions. Tie a bow in the strings making sure it's secure (you don't need this coming undone in the middle of class). Next put on the jacket. Place the right lapel under the left before putting on the belt. Finally, put on your belt. The

correct way of putting of your belt will result in a triangular knot at your tanden (please refer to the following diagrams).

As a final note on the dogi, make sure that you wash it after a day's keiko (practice). If you cannot do this the same day, do not stuff it into your gi bag until you can. Hang it out in the fresh air until you can wash it, or if you are not a person that perspires a lot, this may be enough for a couple more practices. In any case, be aware that the human body sweats, man or woman, and in different amounts. So be conscious of the fact that your gi is going to get to the point of smelling foul if it is not washed after being worn. Keeping your gi clean is not only courteous to the others, but the practice of misogi (cleansing mind and body) teaches us that it is the right thing to do. Remember -- We strive to be defensive, not offensive.

What about the *Hakama*? Why is it so important? What does it symbolize? The following is an excerpt from a small article written by Mitsugi Saotome. "In many ways the wearing of the Hakama has degenerated into merely a symbol of rank, but it actually has a very deep spiritual meaning."

The traditional costume of the Samurai warrior was the joining of two triangles. As you can see in the following diagram,

the upper-most triangle opens toward heaven and symbolizes the spiritual world. The lower triangle extends to earth, making a broad and stable base, symbolizing the physical world. These two triangles are joined at the "hara" -- heaven and earth united in the human body.

The physical and spiritual are one. Therefore, each affects the other. The way we speak and move, our facial expressions, even our manner of dress affects our attitude and our spiritual vibrations. We must embody the "Way", the Universal concepts in movement, in costume, and in everyday life training to keep the Way before us in all our endeavors. O'Sensei said, "The Way means to be one with the will of God and practice it. If you are even slightly apart from it, it is no longer the Way."

Typically, in the United States it has become the custom to wear the hakama after reaching the rank of Shodan (1st Degree Black Belt). It is generally accepted that the male student will not wear the hakama until attaining the rank of Shodan. However, this is not always the case for female students. There doesn't seem to be any universal consistency here, so as a result, you will sometimes find women of all ranks wearing hakamas. The decision is up to the individual dojo sensei and the student herself.

The accepted way of wearing the hakama varies from dojo to dojo. The background of the Chief Instructor determines the accepted way. So all students must realize that if you visit another dojo and see everyone wearing a hakama, you have not necessarily found a large gathering of yudansha; this may be the accepted way for all students at this dojo. Respect the way of the dojo, and do not pass judgment on wearing or not wearing the hakama.

Cleaning the hakama is just as important as cleaning the gi. Although the hakama is an outer garment, it will still get sweaty and dirty. It too, will eventually get to the point of smelling foul if not aired out regularly. As you learn over time, the cleaning of the hakama does not have to be done nearly as often as the gi. As a matter of fact, if you air it out regularly, the hakama need only be cleaned about once every six months. The best way to clean it is to get it dry cleaned. It costs very little and they will press the pleats for you also. In addition, some hakamas have a cardboard piece in the backboard and if you get this wet it will disintegrate or get out of shape. The most durable backboards are made of rubber. You'll also find some made out of felt and these can be damaged also by washing in a machine. Along this same thought, it is very unbecoming to see a hakama (especially all-cotton) that has just come from being stuffed in a gi bag, as they usually appear very wrinkled if not folded well. So take care when cleaning and stowing your hakama (or gi) in your gi bag.

When buying a hakama there are a few suggestions we can make. First, consult your sensei for a source and seek his advice for length specifications, because no matter what is said in this section, your sensei's wishes should take precendence. In any case, the first consideration is the length, which should be such that when the final knot is tied in front, the bottom of the hakama is about an inch off the floor. This fashion will vary greatly, but seems to be the most popular and functional way of wearing it. A caution here is probably in order. Please do not tie your hakama knot in the back. Tying it in this way has been known to cause serious injury to people when taking hard ukemi (falls). Besides that, the knot will not be conducive to the feeling of centeredness. Another consideration is the length of the belts.

The back belts are not quite as important when it comes to length, but the front belts should be long enough to go around you at least twice and then have enough left over to make a nice neat knot at your tanden. This of course will depend on your own physical shape, so you will have to make sure of this measurement yourself. Black and dark blue are the most common colors for the hakama in Aikido.

Folding your hakama or your sensei's hakama is an art that should not be taken lightly. One should take extreme care to fold the hakama very neatly. (Special Note: The day just may come when you are asked to fold the hakama of a prominent instructor and every student should be ready to do a good job of it). We thought about including a diagram of how to fold the hakama in the book, however, we felt there are too many details to be looked after. So we suggest that you ask your sensei or an advanced student to take the time to show you how to fold the hakama. Take particular care when folding the pleats and make sure all corners are square. Make sure all belts lay flat and are folded flat, as this will maintain their shape for a much longer time. If you buy a 100% cotton hakama, be prepared for a lot of wrinkles, so take special care when folding these. A blend of 50% polyester and 50% cotton is probably the most popular because of the wrinkle-free nature of the material. Also, the blended material is not so apt to tear as easily. There are many other materials used to produce hakamas, but these will vary just as the color will. Here again, the choice is yours.

Students should always try to wear *zoris* (sandals) to the dojo. The main reason for this is that they can be removed quickly. You should never come to the dojo bare-footed. The mats get dirty enough without each student bringing in more dirt on the bottom of her or his feet. Therefore, try to wear something on your feet that you can get on and off comfortably and quickly. If this is totally impossible then wash your feet before you step on to the mats.

Aikido Weapons

There are many ways in which "practice weapons" are used in Aikido training. O'Sensei used weapons in his Aikido and his uchideshi have continued with this training to this day. The most popular of the weapons that we have come to know as Aikido weapons are the bokken (wooden sword), the jo (wooden staff), and the tanto (wooden knife).

If you practice with a bokken or a jo, then the following paragraphs should help you. First, you should know that not all weapons are created equal. Some of them are manufactured to be hung on the wall. A new student can often feel that he or she has just gotten a good deal on a weapon only to find later, that it has no functional value at all.

The bokken is a wooden sword and should be used as a sword and not as a piece of wood shaped like a sword. It has a handle end that should be held like the handle of a sword. It also has a tip which should be respected as the tip of a sword. (Note: If you don't believe this, don't practice with a bokken). Practicing with a bokken without these sincere considerations will not only give you a completely false idea of weapons training, but will be quite dangerous to yourself and anyone else with whom you train.

The most desireable of all bokkens are those that have been

made from Japanese white oak. This weapon will hold up for a long time regardless of the treatment it gets and what style of weapons training you practice. When purchased, this weapon will come nearly finished, and there are a few things that should be done by you to make it ready for regular practice. Use a fine sandpaper (about 80 grit), to round the rough edges and to smooth the finish. Put some kind of identifying mark on your weapon so that it is not easily mixed up with someone else's weapon. After you have marked it you have two choices; one, if you use the weapon on a regular basis, then you are done, but if you foresee any length of time between the times you are putting your hands all over it, then you may want to put a light coat of wood finishing oil on it. This will be especially true concerning the tips of the weapon because they will have a greater tendancy to dry out.

The preceding suggestions also hold true for the jo. Again, we have found that the most durable jo is the one made from Japanese white oak. As with the bokken you will have to decide whether or not to oil it, because if put on too thick it will start to get sticky.

No matter what kind of wooden weapons you acquire, remember that your weapons will need regular attention, such as sanding to get rid of small splinters. These splinters may not only be dangerous to you, but please consider your training partners. Be courteous to others and keep your weapons in good shape. When there are too many splinters to be repaired or you suspect your weapon has sustained a fracture, use it for fire wood or simply retire it.

One last suggestion on weapons: Get a carrying case for them. These can be purchased or fabricated. They will help keep your weapons protected from the weather. Never leave your weapons in the trunk of a car for any length of time. If you do, you will inevitably find new curves in them, as extreme heat and moisture will definitely distort them.

CHAPTER 8

Mat Survival

Better Training - Physically and Psychologically

Aikido is a physically and mentally vigorous activity. The learning process of Aikido demands the development of great flexibility, strength, endurance and tolerance for pain. Muscle toning and development is the result of dedicated training. Each class should take you to the limits (and a little beyond) of your physical abilities. It is normal for your gi to be soaked with sweat at the end of a class. At a seminar (a special day of three or four classes) you will need at least two clean gis. To the surprise of many, it is quite common for practicioners of other arts to be amazed at the intensity of physical effort expended during an Aikido class. The point is that Aikidoka are athletes and athletes must prepare and maintain their bodies in order to excel in their chosen field.

Jumbi taiso are traditional exercises specifically designed to prepare the body immediately before a training class and are extremely important. They are just as much a part of the Aikido experience as anything else and you must consider them so.

In the beginning jumbi taiso, in whatever form it takes in your dojo, may seem to be a collection of unusual, exotic and perhaps boring contortions. Your eagerness to train and your over-drive adrenalin levels are screaming "Alright already! Enough! Let's do some Aikido!" This is a perpetual problem common to the beginner. The fact is, you are doing Aikido, you just haven't learned to recognize it yet. Jumbi taiso is an act of *misogi*, or cleansing the body and mind. It has many benefits, including: preparing your biological systems for high level performance demands during the rest of the class.

Careful preparation of the body is the most effective method of preventing injury and is basic to all other organized rigorous activities. Successful athletes do not play or train "cold" and neither should the wise Aikidoka.

Like most things in life, you will receive rewards in direct proportion to the amount of energy you invest. If you have paid proper attention to your jumbi taiso, the results will be a feeling of warmth in your muscles and a light sweat on your body. The musclar tensions of the day will have gone and you will feel a readiness to proceed. Mentally, or spiritually if you prefer, extraneous thoughts will be swept aside. Your attention will be focused in the reality of Aikido and you will experience a hightened sensory awareness of your self, the dojo, your instructor, and your fellow students. This is the beginning of zanshin, the proper mental and spiritual state of the warrior.

To achieve true zanshin is the goal of the serious Aikidoka. It is not a simple thing. Be prepared to start now and spend the rest of your life in the development of this higher reality. Remember, the greatest opponent you will ever face on the Aikido mat (which is often, if not always, an allegory for life in general) is yourself. Freedom from your own self-imposed barriers is the growth and the reward of serious Aikido training. Eventually, jumbi taiso will become a part of your natural behavior pattern. The movements will be rational and meaningful. This will signify your first major step away from the beginning point.

The next element of Mat Survival, which relates to you personally, is your *ukemi* practice. Ukemi is the Art of Defensive Falling. The trained *uke* is a person who has added an entire dimension of movement to his or her repertoire; movement through the horizontal plane. Ukemi teaches a sense of body awareness like that enjoyed by gymnasts. The serious ukemi student becomes a very difficult person to attack successfully. This is a direct result of their increased ability to move in all directions and their developing zanshin. Ukemi practice also brings with it other important benefits; it provides physical conditioning of the body, teaches the fundamentals of rational movement, builds self-confidence, and is essential to all future learning in Aikido. If you listen around the dojo, you will quickly learn that Aikido students have great respect for individuals known as good ukes. In fact, for kyu ranks, ukemi ability is probably the single most important criteria for judging the seriousness of students. There is one more very important reason for all of us to dedicate ourselves to improving our ukemi; our responsibility to our fellow students. Without good ukes, true Aikido practice cannot take place. Training is a cooperative process. The ability of the nage to execute techniques properly, with speed and power, is heavily reliant on the uke's ability to take the fall successfully and get back up, ready to attack again. Remember that uke and nage are a team, each doing his or her part, each helping the other along the path of learning.

Proficiency in the defensive art of ukemi is the most basic and in many ways one of the most important elements of your new art. Serious students should take advantage of the time before class by engaging in light stretching followed by personal ukemi practice. This *warm-up* ukemi should be done carefully with an orientation towards perfection and refinement of technique rather than speed. Keep in mind that the essence of ukemi is controlled movement. Speed will come with practice and is best accomplished under the direct supervision of your sensei.

Aikido is often referred to as the "Gentle Art." There is truth to this statement, but it can also be misleading to those who are not experienced in actual Aikido training. The term "Gentle" refers to the spirit and intent of the art, its form and true students. It does not refer to the rigors of training or to the effectiveness of the techniques. The intent of Aikido, in its martial or "Budo" aspect, is to defeat an attack quickly and efficiently while causing the minimal possible damage to the attacker in the process. This is the elegance of Aikido. When techniques are performed by one who is proficient in the Art, the movements appear deceptively simple. When Aikido is performed by a Master of the Art, the intentionally deceptive and easy movements are often perceived by non-Aikidoka as "mystical." The results seem "out of joint" with reality. Small, quick, sometimes imperceptible movements of the Master result in potentially devastating effects on the uke. Only Aikido students can know the true reality of these techniques through the rigors of their daily training; thousands of rolls and falls, joint lock after painful joint lock, bruises, aches and strains. Eventually, this conditioning hardens your muscles and increases their flexibility. This, combined with your improved ability to move properly, reduces the number of bruises and pains; but, leaves you with a deep respect for the physical conditioning and preparation necessary for even a relatively low level of proficiency within the Art. The truest understanding of this comes on the day in your training when you are fortunate enough to have the opportunity to stand on the mat with a true Master of Aikido and experience a touch of the awesome power she or he generates. At that point, you will know in the deepest sense of the word, whatever mysticism may be associated with Aikido, you have just experienced one of the realist things in your life. You will immediately acquire a brand new appreciation for the importance of preparation and conditioning of your body. You will know with absolute certainty that the word "Gentle" applies to the intent of the Master, and that is the only reason you were able to get back up and continue the class. Endurance, speed, agility and attitude coupled with the rational movement of properly executed technique are the elemental components of Aikido training. Physical and mental fitness is essential.

Thus far, we have spoken of mat survival only as it pertains to one's own responsibilities and actions. Remember that we have said that Aikido training manifests itself physically as a cooperative relationship between uke and nage. The refinement of the cooperative relationship is part of the inner learning experience of Aikido. It is important to remember at all times that what we are cooperating to learn are highly effective, potentially lethal, combat techniques. While it is true that cooperation demands a certain level of mutual trust, it is also true that the ultimate purpose of Aikido is to enhance our defensive control of our own environment. We can only resolve this seeming paradox with careful rational thought. An appropriate analogy may be found in driving an automobile on the open road. Certainly there are rules; speed limits, stop signs and such. But only a suicidal fool makes driving decisions based on an implicit trust that the other driver will obey all the rules or has your best interests in mind at all. The same is true on the mat. Give everyone the respect of trust, at least until they prove themselves incapable or unworthy; but never, ever lower your personal defense or your control of your technique irresponsibly. That is, do not knowingly push your ukes beyond the limits of their ability to protect themselves. Never give a nage a *second* opportunity to use *you* irresponsibly, whether through ignorance or malice.

There can be many interpretations of the concept of cooperation, and because Aikido is practiced by people, people subject to all the possible human frailties, you must be prepared to find less than the ideal. The harder you train, the less relevant this will become.

Let's take a look at some situations that you will probably find yourself involved in many times during your training career, by way of example:

Scenario #1

During an Aikido class you find yourself paired up with a student with whom you are not familiar. You quickly realize that your partner is a relatively new student and not as advanced as you. Some indicators may be his or her awkwardness, unfamiliarity with the basic technique, poor ukemi, obvious intimidation, or proclivity to talk during the practice. Assuming that we are all proper, ethical and non-malicious aikidoka, two obvious courses of action present themselves:

1. You can, with all good intentions, decide to practice as hard as you are able to and rely on your training partner to "take care of themselves" or,

2. You can decide that this person is not able to provide you with a rewarding training experience and simply turn-off and cruise through the rest of the session.

While both of these solutions to Scenario #1 are very common, neither is the proper or constructive reaction of a true aikidoka. For the serious student, Scenario #1 presents a wonderful opportunity for learning and growth; a new challenge on your new skills. The statement, Aikido training is a cooperative process, is an absolute. There are no proper exceptions. In this example, as sempai, or the senior partner, the responsibility to make cooperation happen falls heavily upon you. Your challenge is to find a way to work with your partner at a level that is challenging to their abilities. Within this process, you will realize personal learning in self-control, body movement, and refinement of technique. As you progress, you will learn to appreciate the value of these opportunities more and more.

Scenario #2

In this situation you find yourself paired (or perhaps impaired) with a partner who has probably been training longer than you, and knows it. This is the kind of person who will see her or his experience as an advantage over you and will proceed to use you to satisfy his or her own ego needs. Typically, she or he will size you up and then throw you just a little bit too hard, with just a little bit too much muscle. This is, by the way, always a sign of lack of technique and ability on that person's part. The pins will be unnecessarily harsh or brutal. You will know when you are working with this kind of individual. You will learn to sense or feel her or his negativity. The answer to this situation is relatively direct and simple. Once you understand what is taking place, make your best rational decision as to whether or not you can continue with a feeling of confidence in your ability to protect yourself from injury. If the answer is yes; consider the situation as a challenge to your training and strive to prove to yourself that your ukemi really is a defensive art. There is much to be learned about your training and yourself in such an experience.

If the answer is no, simply excuse yourself, thank your partner for the training and avoid this individual, at least for awhile. There is no custom or tradition in Aikido that requires you to allow yourself to be used for anyone's unethical purposes. Make your choice in the best spirit of the philosophy of Aikido as you understand it.

A related situation, a kind of sub-category occurs when the behavior of your partner is similar, but the cause of the behavior is very different. It is common for relatively new students who are beginning to realize their new skills and the awesome power they confer, and who may also be physically strong individuals, to become dangerous on the mat. Not for any negative reason, but as a result of their excitement, high adrenalin level and inexperience. These are good people, and they will learn. But, in the meantime, they are just as potentially dangerous as the malicious individual. Your response, therefore, is the same. Self-defense in the spirit of good training.

Scenario #3

This is the best. In this case, a high-ranked individual (perhaps a Sensei) is your partner. The practice demands all you've got and some more that you did not think you had. Advice? Go for it! This is the ultimate training experience in Aikido. You are totally aware, totally alive, and operating on the upper edge of your total potential. It is an addictive sensation.

Perhaps in some sense, serious Aikido students are addicts. Addicted to the positive experiences, sensations, and growth that are the result of serious training. All in all, it comes down to this: Training should be enjoyable and should always be a learning experience. Tremendous growth can take place on the mat as well as off. Don't ever be fooled into thinking that the mat, itself, is the great equalizer. You should always keep in mind that not everyone is going to practice the way you want them to practice. This is one of the most important ideas you need to realize, and one of the greatest challenges you will face. Remember that these kinds of learning experiences and challenges, turning the negative into the positive, are all an important part of your Aikido training.

CHAPTER 9

Ranking and Promotional Exams

One of the more controversial parts of Aikido is the ranking system and promotional examinations. Although these are probably two of the most misused aspects of our training, they can provide some of the most positive and inspiring experiences for any martial artist.

In Aikido, the ranking system is a means of monitoring our progress as individuals and not as a means of judging ourselves against our peers. It is of utmost importance to maintain a humble attitude towards your rank and never let it be an excuse for poor manners or discourteous behavior towards younger and less experienced students. There should never be a need to ask an instructor about an examination that you have been involved in because you yourself will know whether you are actually at the level at which you have been asked to perform. Also, hopefully, you will have a sensei that will have the heart and courage to tell you that you need more work and are not yet at that level, in other words, fail you for not performing up to par during a test. When students are passed simply to maintain them as students, the process is obviously being badly misused.

Within the art of Aikido today, there are various ranking systems used. In this section, we will try to discuss one system in detail. This, in our opinion, is very similar to most examinations being given today.

Basically, there are only two belts issued to the adult student, the white and the black. Oftentimes, the children's classes will have colored belt systems to offer more incentives. The white belt signifies the beginning student (kyu grades). Typically, you will find six grades of white belt, but the first exam a student takes will be for their 5th Kyu certificate. As you will see, students will work towards their 1st Kyu certificate in preparation for their first black belt test. The promotional test requirements will vary from dojo to dojo in one way or another at this level.

The black belt is reserved for the advanced student. This student has generally practiced the art for three to four years with good consistency and has a good understanding of shugyo. Once you have the basic skills and understanding, you can start to train at a higher level. The belt that is colored black does not necessarily mean you know everything, but rather that you have become competent enough in the art to start to train seriously and understand the essence of Aikido. Unfortunately, for some it means that once they have earned a black belt, they believe they have mastered the art. It seems like such a waste of time and energy to think in this way and to cut back your training and your learning, when in fact you have really only begun.

Typically, you will find there are ten grades of black belt. These go from Shodan (1st Dan) to Judan (10th Dan). As one can imagine, there are very few people ranked as Judan. As far as the hakama is concerned, once a student achieves black belt rank, the hakama becomes part of everyday Aikido attire. This student should take pride in wearing the hakama and treat it as essential gear for training anywhere and for any reason.

Thus, the black belt and the hakama have become indicative of not only the advanced student, but also the instructor rank. Obviously, anyone can teach what they have learned, but it is generally accepted that the "black belt", also called "yudansha", student be allowed to teach formally. On the other hand, yudansha are never required to become teachers. One of the very fortunate circumstances in a dojo is when you have many higher ranked students who alternate teaching classes. In this setting, the yudansha have the opportunity to act as students, besides teaching, thus keeping their respective egos in check. However, often this is not possible, as others continually seek to have the most advanced students do the teaching.

There are several important titles that everyone should know about when referring to instructors, whether or not they apply to your instructor. The first is the term "Sensei", which means teacher or one that has gone before you.

Special Note: Many students have asked, "What should I call my teacher? Do I call him by name? Or what?"

When you come into a dojo, and there is a *Chief Instructor,* in other words, there is a dojo *Sensei,* you should know his or her name for sure, however, you should call him or her *Sensei* then and forever. This is basic Japanese "protocol." When a teacher has earned the title of Sensei, you, as a student, should refer to him or her as such on or off the mat, in or out of the dojo. (For a further discussion of this, see Appendix A).

It is polite for you to refer to any teacher of Aikido as Sensei instead of by name unless you outrank that person. (Some prefer to reserve this title for their personal teacher alone). In either case, one should be careful to treat any instructor with respect.

A student having attained the rank of Nidan (2nd Dan) will typically be given the title of *Fuku Shidoin* or Assistant Instructor if presently teaching. An instructor having attained the rank of Sandan (3rd Dan) to Godan (5th Dan) willl usually be given the title of *Shidoin*. Once the instructor attains the rank of Rokudan (6th Dan), the instructor is honored with the title of Shihan or master teacher. (Note: When O'Sensei was alive, this was the rank at which he would *graduate* a student). There are quite a few people with the title of *Shihan,* although the numbers drop dramatically once beyond 7th and 8th Dan.

One can see that in Aikido there is definitely a hierarchy of sorts within its structure. We honor the students who have gone before us because without their suffering and mistakes, we would have to train at a lower level. Instead, because of their hard work, we can benefit from their teaching and their having learned better ways of training. We honor the students who have trained with O'Sensei in a special way, also, because with them, there still exists a line to the man who invented what we know today as Aikido. Lastly, we honor O'Sensei at every practice for creating an art form, a budo, that in itself teaches harmony and caring for nature and the natural ways of the universe.

Promotional Examinations

There are basically three ways to be promoted within the ranks of Aikido. The first and most popularly used, up to the rank of Yondan (4th Dan), is the actual test—a physical test of a student's technical skill and endurance under pressure. The second method used is a promotion by recommendation. This is usually done when a student is older or has a physical condition which handicaps the student from the rigors of a physical test. The third way is made up of a combination of the first two.

Let's look at the first method of promoting. The "physical test" is generally the accepted way for all Kyu grades to be promoted. There have been instances where Shodan has been given by recommendation, but these are far and few between, and usually involve extenuating circumstances such as age or physical handicap. Above the rank of Sandan, one will find that recommendations are mostly used, because by this time a student will have been a teacher of some sort, practicing diligently, so objective exams will become academic. A promotion to a higher rank at this level will simply be a matter of dedication to one's study and time contributed to enhancing and spreading of Aikido.

Promotional examinations are given in a variety of ways, and here again we remind you that this book cannot hope to be so comprehensive as to cover all ways, so we will describe one of the most popular ways and the etiquette that goes along with it. In any test there are required techniques that a student must demonstrate to the examining sensei or panel of senseis, in front of the remaining student body. These must be adequately demonstrated and shown to be effective in the way they are used.

The very first step in taking an examination is to make application to your sensei for the rank which you wish to test for. In very few cases is a student ever tested out of sequential order. In other words, students will always be required to take the 5th Kyu exam before they take the 4th Kyu exam. Of course, this is up to the examining sensei to decide (here again, you can see how this system could and has invariably been misused.) After your application has been accepted by your sensei, you will then be scheduled to test on a given day and time.

On the day of your exam, it is wise not to go crazy and work on everything for which you will be tested. If you don't know something that will be required at this time, there is no way you are going to learn it on the same day. So take it easy and rest as much as possible. However, if you really feel strong about it, get a partner to help you walk through techniques and quiz you on the terminology.

When you arrive at class on the day of your exam, try to relax and put the test out of your mind for the time being. Practice as you would normally and pay strict attention to what is going on. In many dojos, the sensei will practice what is to be on the examinations during the regular class, giving hints on how best to demonstrate the techniques. Of course, you should be aware of this since you will be demonstrating your skill to the sensei.

The test will usually be given at the end of the class so that you are fully warmed up and stretched out. After class, the sensei will usually hold a short break so that paperwork can be handled and all senseis who are to participate in the exams can be organized. Once the class has been called to order again, make sure you have already been seated and above all, expect to be called first. If you are not, then be ready to go second. Pay strict attention to what goes on in the test before you and heed any suggestions that might be given by the senseis. When it is your turn to be examined, your name will be called and you should follow the basic rules of etiquette:

1. When your name is called, immediately perform zarei (sitting bow) and then stand and approach the kamiza.

2. Take a seat in seiza position at the kamiza facing the picture of O'Sensei and wait for instructions from the sensei conducting the exam. (Remember, the way you perform your bow sets the mood and attitude of your test.)

3. At this time, the examining sensei may or may not select a uke for you. If so, the uke will take a seat to your right and just behind you. (Note for the uke: When your name is called, immediately perform zarei, stand, approach the position just described and ready yourself to take ukemi for the exam. When the person being tested performs zarei to the picture of O'Sensei, etc. be prepared to follow the lead, don't go any faster or slower).

4. Once your uke is seated, you can begin your test. First perform zarei to the picture of O'Sensei (Note: This is your test, so you lead this ceremonious bow, as your uke will follow); next, turn to your sensei and again perform zarei; now turn to your uke and perform zarei.

5. The examining instructor will then ask for a demonstration of the required techniques. These may or may not be in the order listed on any sheet, so don't be surprised. Be acutely attentive to what your sensei asks for and then perform what is asked. Do not try to be innovative at this

point, but if you make a mistake, always carry through with it. *Don't stop and start over again!* This is a mark of readiness and demonstrates your ability to work under pressure and to adapt to the situation. After all, you may not have been able to demonstrate the given technique because of the way your uke attacked. Don't ever apologize for any mistake you may make during the test. After all, you can't expect to be perfect, so why be sorry when you are doing your best.

6. Once the formal test has been given, each of the assisting senseis will have a chance to ask of you something that may or may not have been on the test that the sensei thinks you should know. This addition could be something that the teacher would like to see you perform over again if you did not perform it adequately the first time around. Be prepared for anything and attempt, to the best of your ability, anything that may be asked of you. Do not hesitate!

7. After all the assisting instructors have had their turn, the test will have been completed.

8. At this point you should be very tired and it is very important to maintain your composure. Adjust your gi to look neat and then take a seat at the kamiza. Face your ukes at this time. Wait for all the ukes to be seated and to have adjusted their gis. When all is ready, perform zarei to them at your leisure; turn to your sensei and perform zarei. If all the senseis are seated together, one bow to them will suffice. However, one of the authors has experienced a situation where each of four instructors was in a different corner of the dojo. In this case, you

would bow to each sensei unless otherwise instructed; finally, turn back to the kamiza and perform zarei to the picture of O'Sensei. Stand and return to your seat among the rest of the class.

When all tests have been completed, the class will typically be closed by the Chief Instructor of the dojo. Some dojos will have the senseis convene for a meeting to discuss passage or failure of each student. In many cases, the results of these meetings will be announced directly afterwards. Other times, the results will not be made known immediately, and the students will have to wait until their names are or are not moved on the nafudakake. In any event, it is not proper to question any of the senseis about your test. *Trust in your senseis at this point is very, very important!*

An important final note about testing: Every student needs to remember the purpose of the examination. The examination is not an attempt to embarrass you, nor is it something to exhibit your extreme superiority over the rest of the student body. The examination is a means for you, as an individual, to become aware of those skills in which you need to work harder. Also, it serves as an indication of the effort that you have been putting into your study.

If by chance you should fail the examination, look at the positive side of the experience. If your sensei feels that you need more basic work on the techniques, then you should heed this and not think anything negative towards the sensei. After all, how would you feel in your heart if you knew that you did not deserve the rank, but your sensei passed you anyway for fear of losing you as a student. If this were the case, what would be the credibility of the exam? What would be the purpose of the exam if you were to be passed without regard to your technical skill? What value would a false assessment of your skill level be to you and to your peers? Trust your sensei as your friend and teacher. Have faith that by testing under your sensei, that you are still being given a lesson.

Examinations in Aikido are going to vary from dojo to dojo. This example is merely one of the many ways, but it is a very popular way of conducting an exam as experienced by the authors. In any case, when considering the Aikido examination, find out all the details of etiquette and requirements well ahead of time. Do not wait until the day of the exam and have to experience the embarrassment of having to ask about something that everyone should know!

Examples of Promotional Examinations Requirements

5th Kyu

1. Shomen uchi ikkyo (omote and ura)

2. Shomen uchi irimi nage

3. Katate tori shiho nage (omote and ura)

4. Mune tsuki kote geaeshi

5. Ryote tori tenshi nage

6. Usiro tekubi tori kote geaeshi

7. Morote tori kokyu ho

4th Kyu

1. Shomen uchi nikkyo (omote and ura)

2. Yokomen uchi shiho nage (omote and ura)

3. Mune tsuki irimi nage

4. Usiro tekubi tori sankyo (omote and ura)

5. Usiro ryokata tori kote gaeshi

6. Suwari waza: Shomen uchi ikkyo, Kata tori nikkyo, Kata tori sankyo

7. Any of the 5th kyu techniques

3rd Kyu

1. Yokomen uchi irimi nage (2 ways)

2. Yokomen uchi kote gaeshi

3. Mune tsuki kaiten nage

4. Usiro ryokata tori sankyo (omote and ura)

5. Morote tori irimi nage (2 ways)

6. Shomen uchi sankyo (omote and ura)

7. Suwari waza: Shomen uchi irimi nage, Shomen uchi nikkyo

8. Hanmi handachi: Katate tori shiho nage, Katate tori kaiten nage, uchi and soto mawari* (see the end of chapter)

9. 13 Jo kata

10. Happo giri (bokken)

11. Any of the 4th kyu techniques

2nd Kyu

1. Shomen uchi shiho nage and kaiten nage

2. Yokomen ichi dai gokyo

3. Usiro tekubi tori shiho nage and juji nage

4. Usiro kubishime koshi nage

5. Morote tori nikkyo

6. Hanmi handachi: Shomen uchi irimi nage, Katate tori nikkyo, Yokomen uchi kote geashi

7. 31 Jo kate

8. 10 Bokken Suburi

9. One uke randori

10. Any of the 3rd kyu techniques

1st Kyu

1. Kata tori men uchi (5 techniques)

2. Yokomen uchi (5 techniques)

3. Morote tori (5 techniques)

4. Shomen uchi (5 techniques)

5. Ryote tori (5 techniques)

6. Koshi nage (5 techniques)

7. Tanto tori

8. Hanmi handachi usiro waza (5 techniques)

9. 6 Kumi jo

10. 6 Awase and ki musubi no tachi (bokken)

11. Two uke randori

12. Any of the 2nd kyu techniques

Shodan

1. All of the 1st kyu requirements

2. Tachi tori

3. Jo tori

4. Henka waza** (see the end of the chapter)

5. 10 Kumi jo

6. 7 Kumi tachi

7. Three uke randori

Nidan

1. Attend 2 seminars per year after Shodan

2. All of Shodan requirements

3. Tachitori w/2 ukes

4. 5 Uke randori

5. Kaeshi waza*** (see the end of the chapter)

Sandan

1. Attend 2 seminars per year after Nidan. Subject matter of this exam to be determined by examiner at the time of exam.

* 　Uchi & Soto Mawari - inside (uchi) and outside (soto) movements

** 　Henka waza - switching from one technique to another, examiner will call first technique

*** Kaishi waza - counter techniques. Uke applies technique to nage. First technique called by examiner, i.e., sankyo against nikkyo.

Aikido in Perspective

When you become a student of Aikido, you also become a member of an international community. This community extends to dojos throughout the world. It consists of thousands of your fellow students. Because we have chosen to study Aikido, we have much in common with other members of this community. As a group, these commonalities set us apart, perhaps most especially from practitioners of other martial arts. These differences will become increasingly apparent to you in the areas of attitude, purpose, and method. Of course, we believe our ways are superior, that is why we remain Aikidoka. In spite of our commonality, there are within the Aikido community, great differences of opinion, attitude and interpretation. It is important that we recognize these differences and make every attempt to understand them and to learn from them. It is also very important to keep a sense of perspective. We are talking about differences between people, all of whom are doing their best to follow the path of O'Sensei. This means that the greatest of differences should be accepted with the tolerance and good faith reserved for family and close friends. For the beginner, the questions arising from the differences with Aikido are often most perplexing and difficult to answer. In order to better understand this problem, we must begin by looking at Aikido from the outside.

In our society, Aikido is one of the large variety of Eastern Martial Arts. For the most part, these Martial Arts are known almost generically, although quite incorrectly, as Karate or Kung Fu. Movies featuring Martial Arts of any type are commonly referred to as *Karate Movies.* For example, how many people know that the character of *Billy Jack,* a movie which helped popularize Oriental Martial Arts in America, actually employed the Korean Art of Hapkido and not Karate? Not many, probably. The point here is that this general identification with Karate tends to make Aikido look small and exotic. The name, the rather strict adherence to Japanese custom in dress, language and protocol, all act to reinforce this exotic nature. Statements such as "Aikido utilizes no blocks, punches, or kicks," tend to add to the mystery and confusion surrounding the Art. Ask around, many people have heard the name Aikido, but few will have any real knowledge about it. Outsiders see Aikido as small and cohesive, while insiders (students) see it as large and diverse. This dichotomy is a fundamental cause of confusion and questioning for new Aikido students.

A major barrier to understanding comes when students try to reconcile the two aspects of Aikido into one comprehensive view. This process does not yield successful results in this instance because both viewpoints are different and both are true. One is not more correct than the other, and neither can be subverted. Understanding can only come when the student's awareness grows large enough to encompass and accept all the aspects of Aikido. This is a learning process. It is difficult, takes a great deal of time, and requires enormous effort on our part. Remember, if Aikido were easy to learn, easy to do, and easy to understand, it would by its own nature be of limited value. It is precisely because of its complexity and the resulting difficulty in learning even the most fundamental precepts that we find it to be of such profound importance in our lives.

The learning process inevitably begins with the students trying to fit themselves into the Aikido world and fit Aikido into the rest of the world. This produces some very important questions for which we shall attempt to provide at least partial answers. These questions we often verbalize in many different ways. However, most of them are variations of the three basic questions. The first is: "Is there more than one Aikido?" The answer to this question is: "No." Aikido, in its fullest sense is the product of the life experiences and teachings of the Founder, Morihei Ueshiba Sensei. It represents the culmination of the life's work of a most remarkable warrior, philosopher and priest. Aikido is the legacy of O'Sensei and is as singular and unique as a fingerprint.

The second question is: "Is there more than one way to practice Aikido?" The answer to this question is: "Yes!" O'Sensei lived a long and fruitful lifetime during which he taught many students. The best of these personal students were "graduated." This means that they achieved the rank of Rukudan (sixth degree black belt) and were awarded the title, Shihan or Master Teacher. As "graduated" students, they were permitted to take students of their own and encouraged to continue to develop themselves and their art. Many of these Masters did just that and since the passing of O'Sensei in 1969, they have continued to follow this path.

These original students have been instrumental in spreading Aikido throughout the world and are recognized for their achievements and contributions to the Art. Each knew the founder at a different point in the development of Aikido and each has taken his teachings and gone on to develop the Art in his or her own unique and special way. Consequently, today we have many different attitudes affecting the way Aikido is practiced from dojo to dojo.

As part of this second basic question you might ask, "So which way should I study?" or "Which is the best style?" The true answer to either of these questions can only be found within yourself. Beyond its physical manifestations, Aikido is essentially an intensely personal experience. Therefore, the style that is best for you is quite simply the one that feels best to you, the one that provides you with the most personal satisfaction.

To find your way, the authors suggest the following three steps:

1. Train hard, concentrate on the basics. Condition your mind and body. Absorb everything you can from your sensei.

2. As your skill and confidence levels increase; attend seminars, visit other dojos, and train with everyone. Above all, keep an open mind!

3. When you find that special teacher (and this may happen more than once in your career), follow your heart. Do what you feel to be right. Train for yourself first! To do

CHAPTER 10   *Aikido in Perspective*

less is to be dishonest with yourself and your fellow
students.

The third basic question is: "Are there other kinds of Aikido-
like Arts?" "Yes!" Why? Because the martial aspects of Aikido
rest upon a thousand years of Japanese warrior tradition.
O'Sensei did not invent Aikido out of thin air. Rather, he
developed and modified the ancient and time tested battle
techniques of the elite Samurai Warriors into a unique Budo,
designed for the modern world. Historically, the combat disci-
plines encompassed within the general philosophy of "Aiki" can
be traced directly back to the earliest days of Japanese Society.
Known practitioners have included the earliest Shoguns themselves. Therefore, Aikido is directly related to all of the classical
warrior arts of Japan. These abundant similarities and subtle
differences concerning Aikido become increasingly obvious and
meaningful as one's knowledge and understanding of the Art
increases.

The 1980's have seen a growing interest in the historical and
technical relationship between Aikido and other arts. A great
deal of research, much discussion, and a lot of controversy has
thus far resulted. Much is yet to be learned from this process,
but two things are certainly true: Aikido is a living, growing
Budo designed for the modern world; and the physical aspects
of Aikido, as beautiful and awesome as they can be, are only the
outward manifestation of what is most importantly a real and
direct way to improve the quality of our lives.

The diagram on the next page is a chronological listing of the
historical antecedents of modern Aikido and a listing of the
major recognized schools of Aikido.

AIKIJUTSU AND AIKIDO FAMILY TREE

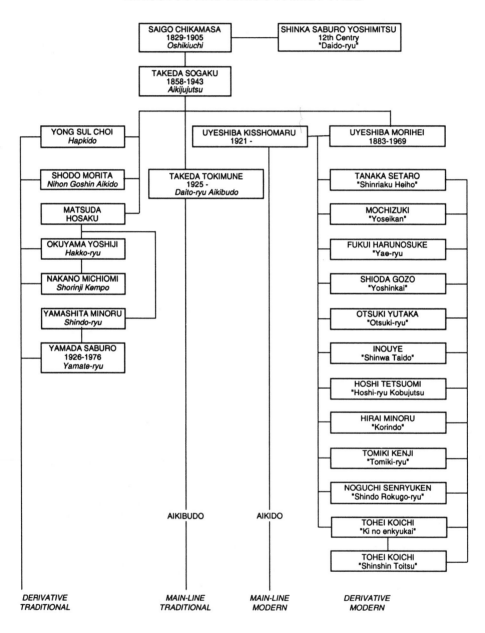

Shihan
Steven Seagal
An Interview

*T*he following are excerpts from an interview with Shihan Steven Seagal. The purpose of the interview was to seek answers to some very difficult questions in an effort by the authors to provide the most definitive information available.

Seagal Sensei offered a wonderful opportunity because of his eminent qualifications; a Sixth Dan Aikido Master, a Shinto Priest in the Omoto Kyo Sect in which O'Sensei himself was a Priest, and an American who has spent most of his life living in Japan and studying Aikido within its true cultural context. Who better an original source for our book? Seagal Sensei is himself a living bridge between Aikido in Japan and Aikido in America.

He is also a very nice man who, like many others we have met in the course of creating this book, graciously offered his time and knowledge and the opportunity to "pick his brain." In a true case of serendipity, one of the authors taped the entire conversation for later reference. When we went back and checked this reference tape, what we found was a concise and elegantly worded discourse on some of the most important and most obscure aspects of Aikido training.

We realized immediately that we had something even more special than we had first thought and that it was a natural part of this book. A part that had to be presented in its original wordings. We also knew that we had to edit our own dumb-sounding questions, and we did. So, with maximal editing of our questions and minimal editing of Seagal Sensei's speaking, we present what we feel deeply is an original and therefore very special addition to this book. For you to read, consider, and ponder as we continue to do . . .

The session opened with Seagal Sensei being asked to elaborate on some comments he had made several days prior to this interview, regarding the subject of protocol in Aikido Training.

SS: Well, the importance to me is they (new students) should understand that protocol is not the same conception that the average Westerner already has. The first important rule that anybody should have in coming into a dojo is to have an empty cup. It is to have no preconceived notions or expectations about what this is. That is to say, protocol to a Westerner, in many instances means some kind of prefabricated, formal ritual that someone has to go through, that doesn't have to do with anything. But highly to the contrary, in essence, protocol in the Japanese sense is the very most basic vehicle created to take you through the numbers of the learning, in what one has to experience in order to reach the goal which is *proper learning*.

What I try to tell my students is that we have to learn how to begin properly. And that in learning how to begin properly, you learn the essence of the protocol. The protocol is starting at the basics. Starting at the basics has to do with absolute humility. Knowing that you know nothing about what is about to go on and that you must become an empty mirror, you know? And when you start with that attitude, you understand that discipline is one of the keys to protocol.

It's like in *tea ceremony,* people see all this superfluous silly movement going on, and they think, God, what a silly waste of time. In reality, tea ceremony and all of those movements, and all of the etiquette and protocol involved is to teach you humility, grace, and tranquility. These are some of the basic elements that are hidden within the secrets of protocol.

All of the values of protocol that I am just discussing with you, are never going to be even discovered by your average Westerner if he or she just gets out there and says OK, I'm going to bow to the shrine, because everybody else is bowing to the shrine. Why do I have to say this . . . and do that . . . you know? But the idea is, the road to enlightenment can . . . Any form of enlightenment can only be achieved through suffering, and through hardships and through overcoming hardships, and overcoming difficulties. In other words, any form of enlightenment can only be obtained when the road to all of one's theoretical progress is blocked. Do you see what I'm saying? Even when the road to thinking . . . a lot of times the teacher will teach by blocking the road to thinking.

And that's the other side of protocol. It's not only all of these things, but it is to create a state of mind so that the students can learn better. And that to me is the essence of protocol.

When a student has had the road to thinking blocked, when he's had all of his senses deprived, in other words, you are starting at the most sparse of levels with everything; there's not a lot of food, there's not a lot of drink, there's not a lot of acceptance, there's not a lot of praise, there's not a lot of any of that. Do you see what I'm saying? Traditionally in the dojo there's none of that.

You know, really it is the most basic of basics. It is one room full of straw mats and a mirror, or straw mats and an altar. When I say mirror, I mean altar. I don't mean the mirror on the walls. And those basics symbolize a form of deprivation of everything other than that. That is to say you are in that room to face, and for the first time, open up and view yourself. That room of deprivation, if you will, is the way to help you to develop a frame of mind where you become so hungry and so attuned and so attentive, because there's nothing else there but that. Now you can learn. That to me is the essence of protocol. Do I make any sense?

Q: Yes. It does, but I am viewing it from my point of view and not so much from the point of someone just walking into the dojo.

SS: Yes . . . I can only give you the whole picture, which is maybe very advanced and anything that you can take out of any of this in the most basic form will be good. I can tell you what I can tell you, and you can maybe try to find the root form and put some of the broad strokes down on paper.

Q: We believe that's precisely what we're trying to do, however, how can this be expressed to many beginning students in America who are used to a Western Style of learning, which is an analytical, systematic style verses an Eastern Style of learning which is totally different?

SS: Yes. It is the classical catch 22 in the sense that really in Japan students are expected to come into the dojo adhering to basic protocol which basically in the simplest of terms means to sit down, follow orders, follow what everybody else is doing, and listen and pay attention, and *learn* to listen and pay attention and *learn* to learn from what you see and what you hear. And *that* should be in this book.

For a certain period, if the teacher's good, he will see at that certain period that this person has been around long enough to now start to learn some of these things. In other words, if I say "OK, now we are going to do a certain form of jumbi taiso, we are going to do something like, jumbi undo." And, you know, everybody starts going like this (motioning an exercise). And the guy says "Well, what is that for?" You know, on his first day, if I show him what that's for, he probably really is not going to understand, for one thing.

For another thing, if somebody on their first day comes in and wants to ask everything that they don't understand, you're going to be spending the whole day, and every other day teaching them what they don't understand. Whereas, if they, by paying attention, by shutting up, by listening, and watching, and doing; if they figure it out, it is going to be so much more meaningful to them because they are going to understand it on a different level. Do you understand that?

Here again, there's a fine line between how much they are supposed to figure out, and how much you can help them with, or how much you should help them with. And my feeling on that is that a basic book like this in every dojo would be wonderful in the sense that if they read this, they will have a basic knowledge of most of what is going on in the Aikido dojo, however; at the same time, I think a little bit of a description of some of what I'm talking about now in terms of the attitude with which they should enter a dojo would help.

Q: So you see this book as somewhat of a complement, a blending of Eastern and Western learning systems?

SS: That's right. This form of shugyo [Japanese] has been around for two thousand years at least. And it's not around by accident. And what shugyo is all about is not being spoon fed. It's about trying to attune your awareness to being able to really understand and learn by looking, being quiet, listening and doing.

Q: Questions often asked by beginners and spectators of Aikido practice are, "Is he really taking ukemi (falling) out of necessity or is he just falling for convenience; and, is he really be thrown like that?"

SS: It depends on who's throwing him, doesn't it?

Q: An answer often given in the form of a question is "What is reality?" How would you react to this as a question?

SS: I'll tell you exactly what I'd say. I'd say two things. I'd say one, it depends on who is throwing whom. And I would say two, right now if I'm throwing Matsuoka (Chief Instructor of the Tenshin Dojo), yes it's real. And I would say right now if I'm throwing Larry, it's real.

I would say, on the other hand, if I'm throwing a beginning white belt, most of the time it is real, and I'll tell you why. Even though they are an utmost beginner, and even though we can't get to the real thing together, we are still . . . I'm trying to find their level of confidence and fit that and go seriously at that level. That is to say, I am not going to throw them or do any joint lock or any strikes or anything to the point where they are really going to get hurt unless they understand this and want to go harder.

I've been in classes with beginners in Aikido that were advanced in other arts that wanted to test me and saying "Well, this doesn't really work" and "I'm going to do this" and I've had somebody dislocate their own shoulder completely out. I had him and he tried to flip his body out of it, and he just dislocated his arm right out.

Q: So practice, then, is a series of progressive approximations of reality and sometimes they reach reality?

SS: Well, to be perfectly brutal, I don't really like the way you are wording that. Only in the sense that . . . I mean it's true, but it's going to give people the wrong idea. That is to say, here again, it is real. All the way when you're really practicing Aikido on the mats with me, it's real no matter who I'm with any time.

The difference is when you're able to practice it at a high enough level, you can't get into something that is more, you know, no holds barred. In other words, you don't have to restrain yourself from going into the things that are more dangerous. It's real in the sense that no matter how much a beginner you are on the mats, if you do the wrong thing, you're going to get hurt.

If a beginning person comes up to me and he says, "I bet I can hit you in the face" and he hits me in the face, there is a chance that that person might end up on their head and they might not know how to fall. There's another chance that they'll end up softly down on their back without getting hurt.

Q: So they are not approximations of reality, but rather; they are reality based on the student's own ability?

SS: They are real .. different levels of reality, exactly, see the difference? The key phrase is, "It is all your level of ability." O'Sensei was known to always have said, "Ai te no chikara awasu", and what this means, loosely translated, is that you have to practice at the ability of your partner, and it always has to be the stronger and more adept person that has to adjust to the less adept, for obvious reasons. If I try to go as hard as I can with you, Joe, you're probably going to die, you know what I mean?

Q: Yes!

SS: And I don't think that anybody should ever think that just because I am practicing with a 14-year-old kid out there that I'm not doing real Aikido or that this kid is not doing real Aikido. Because, it is real Aikido! They're doing the very best that they can.

When we talk about levels of adeptness, that's a different story, but the same thing does hold true. When somebody's trying as hard as they can to punch you, and trying as hard as they can to do the technique right, I'm trying as hard as I can too, to do Aikido with them, no matter what level it is.

The ugly reality is, and it is just as beautiful as it is ugly, is this . . . in Japan, as you now well know, for the first two years that I had my dojo, forgetting about problems that I had with the mafia, yakuza, or anything else, because I was the only caucasian that had taught in Japan, I had people every day, trying to, what

Westerners would call . . . getting a cheap shot or hit me from behind, whatever, trick me, get one in on me.

Quite frankly, even if I wasn't white, there is a tradition among serious Martial Artists, that is to say, if you don't demand a real situation, a real atmosphere in your dojo, where people are able to go hard, and they do go hard, then your practice becomes, in my opinion ineffective. Like, for instance when somebody in an Aikido dojo says OK . . . and they stop here (pointing to the end of his nose). They go to punch you and they'll stop before they hit you.

When you attack me you better come to really grab me, you better come to really punch me, you better come to really kick me, or I'll get really upset, because then, you are ruining Aikido, you are ruining the practice, and then yes; there is no reality, and there is then a different approximation of reality because you are playing games. Am I making sense?

Q: Yes.

SS: The only other thing that I can say here is that traditionally in other dojos, you'll find a lot of different teachers trying a lot of different things a lot of different ways. It takes time for the beginner, in order not to get hurt, to be able to go full-bore at Aikido. It does not mean that before he can go full-bore that he is not serious and that he's not trying as hard as he can, or that what he is doing is invalid in any way.

In other words, somebody might be able to punch me and kick me as fast as anybody, but he can't take the fall afterwards. So, because of that we have to alter the practice. What it is, is that we have to adjust to the strength and the level and the different aspects of levels of ability of the student. It is back to "Ai te no chikara awasu."

Now maybe he's a great Karate Shodan and a great fighter, but maybe he just can't take the falls. So I'm not going to be able to throw him, or I'm going to hurt him. This doesn't mean to say that he's not going to be able to attack me seriously either. The only thing that a student like that shouldn't do is; they shouldn't try to sneak up on somebody and give them the best they have from behind or whatever, because then you don't necessarily know who it is behind you and you go to throw him or her, you know what I mean I mean there are situations where they have to be careful.

Q: How do you explain many Martial Arts dojos (Aikido as well as others) where it seems the training is so rehearsed and so compromising? Sometimes it seems, the only reason an instructor has students is to make a buck and to have a social club.

SS: Well, my feeling is that basically, and I wish you'd quote me, what has traditionally happened a lot, is certain people, some very famous, have been overseas, in the service. And maybe they studied six months to two years of a martial art, then they're out of the service. The fact is, it hasn't been two years because they're entire stint was only two years. So in reality, they've only gotten six months of actual martial arts training on the average. They come back to America and maybe they've received a Shodan in Okinawa, automatically they think they're a teacher.

One of the reasons the Japanese never ever wanted to take me seriously is because, and one of the reasons why they felt it was their job to make me quit as Uchideshi, or kick me out of the dojo, or not teach me, was because traditionally this is the way

Americans have been, and other foreigners had been. They come over, they learn six months or a year of a martial art, they think (snap) they are a teacher, and they think that they know it all when they haven't even scratched the surface yet.

Then they come back to America and they start teaching. What I'm really trying to say is the martial arts have, generally speaking, been born wrong in America. Aikido generally speaking has been born wrong in the sense that some of the teachers, maybe a lot of the teachers didn't really get their basics down before they started teaching.

When I go from dojo to dojo, sometimes for example; I see people attacking each other and then I see the Uke falling before he's even been thrown, falling before he's even touched. How could this possibly have anything to do with Aikido? O'Sensei always said "Aikido wa budo de aru." And what I felt he really meant was, "This is a martial art and if it doesn't work, take up aerobics, take up dance, or take up a gun! But don't call it the Martial Arts." Aikido is a Martial Art. OK? I think that there are Aikido dojos in America that have damaged the name of Aikido and many of my different friends that I respect and are Karate Masters, and Kung Fu Masters, say Gee . . . Even a lot of my students became my students by accident because they had seen Aikido and thought it was a joke. They saw people randomly taking falls for each other.

I think that the two of you here can testify that you've really tried to hit me, and you've really ended up on the mat and you know that it's the real thing because it hurts, and it works.

Basically, what I feel is that you have people practicing like this in many places because they never learned it before in the first place. O'Sensei said that the basics should never change. So when you don't know your basics, and then you try to make it up as you go along, it starts to resemble something that . . . doesn't even resemble Aikido.

O'Sensei always talked about shinken shobu, or fighting to the death, or at least with that feeling. So that if somebody lives, fine, and if somebody dies, that's too bad, either way. It's that seriousness of life or death that's lacking with many people and they end up making it a play. Aikido is not a play.

You know, I used to hear stories of O'Sensei. People were trying to kill him constantly. Many times he was faced with death. Many times people tried to kill him. They didn't try to punch him, they didn't try to throw dirt in his face, they tried to kill him. You know there's a difference. And that's why O'Sensei's Aikido worked.

Q: Will you explain the relationship between love and harmony and the fact that Aikido is a real martial art?

SS: You see, you are talking about one of the most difficult subjects to talk about in the world, right now, in Aikido, and that is yes, Aikido is based on Love, yes it is based on Harmony, yes it is based on Oneness, and yes it is based on not having an enemy. Even if somebody comes to try to cut my throat right now, in my opinion, they're not necessary my enemy, because I have what we call *mushin*. When somebody attacks me I don't think about, I'm going to get him, I'm going to do this. It's just a state of mind, a heart without emotion, a mind without emotion that I have, and the only thing I'd do is react to terminating the situation to the best of my ability.

So a lot of this is philosophy in the way to live your life. To try to live your life in harmony and goodness and oneness, and also a lot of it is not to allow your emotions to affect you in your action, because if you allow your emotions to affect you in your action, you are probably going to lose. A lot of these are techniques, tricks. Techniques to teach you how to have a superior attitude in a time of conflict or attack or war or whatever. Am I making myself clear?

Q: Well, I think so, but what I'm saying is that I think that most of the people I've ever come in contact with that practice Aikido probably either wouldn't or certainly wouldn't want to believe that he (O'Sensei) was a violent person.

SS: I'm not saying that O'Sensei was a violent person at all. Besides, violent is a limited word and in French and in German and in Spanish and in a lot of different languages they have a word that denotes heavy, fast moving action, like in Japanese we say "Hageshi!". Violent sometimes has a negative connotation in English that's attached with something bad. Like when you look at my Aikido you may call it violent. But nobody is necessary getting hurt.

Q: So what would you say to people who don't see it in the practical way that you do, or understand it the way you do?

SS: Well, my answer to that is simply this . . . if you look at the world today, you will understand that the world is not necessarily a fair place. People will trick you any possible way they can, they will shoot you in the back. They will do whatever they can. The world is full of what I call mutations, sick, evil people that will do whatever they can to do whatever they want to you.

It is also full of good people, but God only knows when you are going to meet a good person and when you are going to meet a bad person. All I'm trying to say is that when you are in the street, the reality is that you have to be prepared for the worst and hope for the best. And if you think that you can go out into the street and have somebody come up to hit you from behind with a blackjack on your skull or come up and try to cut your throat, if you think that a philosophical view of peace and love is going to help, then you better wake up, because it's not.

My answer is also, that the world can be a very ruthless, dirty, violent place, and if you cannot bring yourself to the level to be ready for that to the extent with which you are able, then you are living in a dream land. Become a writer and just stay in your house and read fiction all day.

Q: Could you comment on the fact that learning Aikido is a much longer process than in other arts, such as Kenpo Karate? How can we talk about that in terms of a reasoning process for people?

SS: What I've always said is that it is very easy for someone to go like this (blocks head with forearm). Because all their life, when all of a sudden they see a baseball bat coming at their face, the first thing that they do is lift their hand to block it. That's reflexive. It is an animal reflex and it's easy. This is the kind of thing that you are basically starting to learn in Karate, which is a fabulous art and I love it very much.

With Aikido you have to unlearn first. That is why it is so hard. You are learning something that is very, very sophisticated. It is something that Warriors after hundreds and hundreds and hundreds of years of dedicated endeavors, of life and

84

death situations, have finally figured out that there is a point of least resistance, and that there is something that works beyond strength...physical strength. It is Ki, it's attitude and it's adept movements that seem to go beyond force, and that a lot of times using strength is completely secondary to learning a way. A kind of moving without resistance, a non-resistant movement, a relaxed movement.

So you have to unlearn in order to learn. It does take longer. However, I will say that in defense of that as hard as it is to learn, the process by which you learn it is so demanding or different in its demand, physically and mentally, to the point where it is exceptionally rewarding and the benefits you reap from it, physically and mentally, are very different from the other more straight forward arts. You know the stimulation that it gives your brain, the stimulation that it gives your spirit, your emotional levels, and physical state. They are all different, and in my opinion, more rewarding and better.

I could go into specifics here if you want, but that is the basic idea. I mean even just the rolling alone. You don't really roll in Karate and a lot of the other Arts. The rolling alone has deep stimulation to the organs. The lungs, the kidney, the heart, and with that deep stimulation it regenerates the organs and generally makes people much healthier. Just that alone, that's just one of the little things that Aikido has.

Q: I think it would be good if we could say more about that. That is one of the reasons I've seen people turn away without ever giving themselves a chance, because they'll ask the question, "Well, how long is it going to take me to get a black belt?"

SS: I generally take the attitude of a kind of almost

contempt with people like that in the sense that if they're involved in the martial arts to get a black belt, then let them go somewhere and buy one. The benefits that one should reap in the martial arts have nothing to do with the color of a belt, they have to do with developing spiritual awareness, developing mental and emotional calm and strength and developing physical health and things like that. I think you should quote me on that, because that is definitely something that I want to say to the people, that if they want to buy a Black Belt let them go anywhere and buy one. There are plenty of places that are selling them right and left.

Q: I think that there are a lot of people out there who have never had the opportunity to explore this and therefore they don't know enough to not want a black belt right away.

SS: See a carrot on a stick, for all intents and purposes, is generally the way it's put out there by people who want the money, and their sole purpose of teaching the martial arts is for money.

Q: But also, not just money, but students. I mean students translate into money, but the whole idea that we're talking about is people that put out these black belts all over the place are going to have more students. They can generate 10 dojos at 40 students a dojo. And it seems they'd compromise anything to do so.

SS: My advice is to beware of people that are going to tell you that they are going to give you a ranking within any specified time. You have to be aware of the charlatans in the martial arts. One of the telltale signs of the charlatans, and I think that this should be in the book too, is somebody who says "Yes, we will give you so much ranking in so much time" which to me is automatic proof of somebody being a phoney because ranking has to be so personal. Some people will learn certain things in six months, and other people will take six years. There's no way that this can be any other level other than an individual level. It is very personal.

Q: Perhaps it is not the fault of Americans who think in those terms of how to get a black belt. They really want everything else too, they just don't know that there might be a conflict there?

SS: They have to be educated and that's what this book is about.

Q: We also wanted to ask today if you have any comments on what more needs to be included in the book itself. Beyond the specifics of it what are the big areas that haven't been addressed?

SS: Once somebody has the title of Sensei, it is never taken away. Let me elaborate on that. Number one, the political status, the nightmarish political status of Aikido in America has really nothing to do with protocol as is. Protocol in Japan says, once somebody is a Sensei, it is proper protocol to refer to them as Sensei, whether it is on the mats or off the mats, they are always Sensei.

However, protocol also says that if you do not respect that person as Sensei, never call him Sensei, not once not ever. You call him Mister. The other thing that protocol says is that when I am higher ranking than you, and I like you, I can call you Reynosa anyway. That is what protocol says. So if you don't respect so and so, you don't call him Sensei, but if he was what I consider a true Sensei, and he outranks you, you would call him Sensei always. It is like Abe Sensei, I call him on the phone and call him Sensei. He is always Sensei to me. My closest students will always call me Sensei, because that is my title and they respect me as Sensei. Basically speaking, the protocol is that when you are an Aikido Sensei and you are the real thing and people who learn from you, people who are your students will call you Sensei always, and quite frankly, real protocol states that even other people will call you Sensei.

In other words, somebody like an art teacher that I know in Japan, and most of my friends and associates in Japan and my business associates, would call me Sensei because that was my title.

Q: That kind of recognition of the martial arts is part of the Japanese culture and there is really no analog in the American culture. Don't you think it's sometimes very difficult for someone with no background to accept and adjust to this custom.

S: It is a little bit similar, like for example, if somebody is a doctor. A lot of times just generally out of respect you don't walk into the office and say, "Hi, Frank", you say, "Hi Doctor", because he is a doctor and that is his title.

Q: Most dojos seem to have adopted parts of this system. For example, they utilize the term Sensei, on the mat only.

SS: That's because they don't know the protocol. They say "Well, I think I'll dispense with this part of the protocol and I think I'll dispense of this part of it, and that part of it." Pretty soon everyone who didn't really know much about protocol, of the essence of it to begin with, have disposed of so much of the bones of what's happening that you don't have anything left.

When you start taking away from the protocol you start taking away from the history, you start taking away from the bones, the essence. And these people don't know the difference between what is the essence of something and what is the protocol and what's both at the same time.

Q:　So now we are back to the beginning. Adhere to the system without any analyzing. Just accept the system and conform within it?

SS:　That's right. When you get to a point where you start to understand the basics, then you can come and analyze and start asking questions and try to put it together so that you understand on a deeper level. But in the beginning if you come up and you just start asking where, why, what to everything, number one you are not going to understand it on a deep enough level to retain it . . . you don't even have the understanding to ask it.

Q:　Different instructors get tied up in trying to answer these questions and soon it seems they start compromising instead of admitting their lack of knowledge and searching for the answers.

SS:　Which you should not be doing. You lose everything. You lose the essence of what is happening. There really should be no compromising. There has to be some form of inevitable adaptation. But even that you have to be ever so careful with. You don't want to give much quarter at all. The only adaptation you make is things that you have to for the betterment of the art, not for its detriment. There is an old joke in Japan, they say "What's an American?", and the answer you hear is "Why do you want to know?" Students always want to ask why. I've said that many times, when I've been asked certain questions. I'd say, "I'd like to answer that question in six months or a year or whatever." It has nothing to do with "my way" or "our way" really.

Q: Sensei, what do you feel are important purposes for beginning Aikido study?

SS: Developing spiritual awareness, the perfecting of the physical man, the developing and nurturing of the emotional and mental and psychological state of man, the nurturing and developing and helping the physical state of man, the medical state of man, a lot of people have been cured by this so it helps you become a healthy person physically. It helps you become healthy and well-balanced mentally, psychologically, emotionally and it helps you develop and perfect your spiritual awareness.

Q: What if somebody wants to learn to fight?

SS: It will teach you how to not fight. It will teach you to defend yourself. But if you want to learn how to hurt people, and be offensive, I think that if you have any kind of teacher at all, you are going to end up changing your attitude or leaving the dojo. Another thing that is real difficult to talk about is, in my opinion, O'Sensei founded Aikido, he invented Aikido. If I invented a sprinkler and I want to call it a sprinkler, it is called a sprinkler. Harold Schmedlap can't take it away from me if I have it patented and everybody knows I invented it. He can't steal it from me and call it a Schmedlap, because it is not fair and it is not right, and it is not true. Some have perverted the art of Aikido, changed it and yet they still use the name. Some did that to an extraordinary degree. These are more difficult politics that are hard to talk about but true.

The point is, O'Sensei's Aikido, and you can quote me on this too, you can say "In Steve Seagal's opinion . . ." there are no styles of Aikido. There is only one Aikido. And that is O'Sensei's Aikido because he invented it. And the other people who learned a little bit from him went off and formed their own art are doing something that may resemble Aikido in one way or another, but it is not Aikido. It is something else. It is a different version of it, that in many instances is what I would describe as a poor bastardization as such. If you want to attack the issue of . . . What people are calling jumbi taiso is actually originally called gyo, which means a kind of religious, austere training. Gyu, shugyo no gyu and ama no tori fune has to do with an ancient style of religious Shinto Purification Rituals.

O'Sensei, you just have to admit was a Mystic and a very religious man. He felt that Kotodama, which is the study of holy sounds and holy words, was the deepest secret of Aikido. He felt that by us practicing the gyo, before we did Aikido, it would remain a holy art which it should be because of its nature, no punching, blocking, kicking in accord with God and the universe. Ama no tori fune literally means: Ama means heaven; no tori fune means like the bird boat, or the floating boat, like you are rowing through the different spiritual realms in heaven.

I don't know if you can even put this stuff down. Ama no tori fune, this exercise was written by Deguchi Onisaburo and some of the old, great Shinto Mystics. It is one of the oldest and purist purification rituals known to man. Just this movement alone (clasps hands in front of his hara and makes a slight up and down motion). So what he did was along with the clapping and the sounds, this was supposed to make a sound of *ta . . . ta ka ama hara no to*. It is a holy sound having to do with Heaven.

Here again, *e sa, sa e* and pulling in the energy, extending the energy, going through these religious ceremonies and these mystical rights is that they're supposed to put you in a spiritual atonement and spiritual attitude before you start doing Aikido. It is a pure form of meditation. The equivalent would be doing certain religious mudras and mantras before you begin Aikido in the Indian sense. That's the easiest way I can explain that to you and explain that to the people that read it.

Q: What about clapping, the clapping is different. Some people will clap twice, some four times?

SS: Let me tell you about that too. O'Sensei was a Priest in Omoto Kyo, as I am. I know the law there. When you have an Omoto Kyo altar, you clap four times, because that's God. You really shouldn't clap to O'Sensei unless you are doing *tsukinamisai,* which is a monthly *matsuri,* a big religious ceremony, or *ireisai,* which is once a year. On the day O'Sensei died, you do a special religious ceremony where you commune with his spirit and pay homage to him. That's the only time you clap twice to him.

Really, if you have him enshrined, which we don't in my dojo ... When you do that you have a straw effigy of him, you call his spirit into this little box and you keep it there. This is all real Shinto Doctrine, it's no joke. That's when you clap twice to O'Sensei every time. When you do not have him enshrined, and you are not doing ireisai and you are not doing matsuri, you don't clap to him twice. That's the real Shinto law. The other people who do other things, they don't understand what they are doing.

Q: What if you have a dojo without an Aiki Shrine?

SS: If you have an Aiki Shrine, you can clap four times in the sense that you can be projecting God there yourself, but really, classically, if you have no shrine at all, other than just a picture of O'Sensei, you should bow once to God and once to O'Sensei and there should be no clapping at all. That's the real protocol. Because the clapping is to the Gods, or to an ancestor or someone that is dead.

This concludes the excerpts from our interview with Seagal Sensei.

Shihan Mitsunari Kanai

A Thought on Reigisaho

Translated by Taitetsu Unmo

Fundamental Philosophy of Reigi

The motivating principle of human survival, based upon the instinctual need of food and sex, is power. The ability to effectively use power is crucial for the sustenance of life itself. The technology of fighting, pre-modern and modern, is an expression of this power, and the human race has survived to this point in history because of the ability to properly use this power. In fact, advances, civilization, and culture. The basic principle of power is deeply rooted in life itself, and it is still the basis of human society as we know it today.

Kanai Sensei is the Chief Instructor at the New England Aikikai, located in Cambridge, Massachusetts. Kanai Sensei was uchideshi of O'Sensei for many years and is presently ranked 7th Dan. Kanai Sensei is not only an expert in Aikido, but is also an expert in the Art of Iaido (Sword drawing).

The student of Aikido, regardless of the reason, has chosen this particular form of martial arts as his or her path, seeking to integrate it into daily life and undertaking the practice with dedication and constancy. Some people get enjoyment out of the Aikido training while some others get lost and fall into confusion. Some approach the training selfishly while others approach with modesty. Each person's approach to the training is a personal expression of his or her sufferings and conflicts as a human being. Thus, the person applies his or her own judgment to Aikido and tries to give his or her own meaning to Aikido. The significance of Aikido, first of all, is that it is a martial art, but it also has meanings the manifestation of natural laws and as a psychological, sociological, physiological, ethical, and religious phenomenon. All of these are overlapping, although each has its own unique identity, and together they constitute what we call Aikido.

If we pursue the combative aspect of Aikido in our training, we can find an extremely lethal and destructive power in Aikido. Therefore, if Aikido is misused, it can become a martial art of incomparable danger. Originally, martial arts meant this dangerous aspect. Aikido is no exception. Thus, any combative art unaccompanied by a strict philosophical discipline of life and death is nothing but a competitive sport.

While sports do not deal directly with life-or-death situations, they nevertheless advocate certain values necessary for the building of character; for example, the observance of rules, respect for other, sportsmanship, proper dress and manners. This should be even more true and essential in the art of Aikido because Aikido deals with the question of life-or-death and insists on the preservation of life. In such an art is it not unquestionably appropriate to emphasize the need of dignified

Rei in human interactions? Therefore, it is said that Rei is the origin and final goal of budo.

Some people may react negatively to this emphasis on etiquette as old-fashioned, conservative, and even feudalistic in some societies, and this is quite understandable. But we must never lose sight of the essence of Rei. Students of Aikido are especially required to appreciate the reason for the meaning of Reigisaho, for it becomes an important step toward misogi, which is at the heart of Aikido practice.

At any rate, people working in martial arts tend to become attached to technical strength. They become arrogant and boorish, bragging of their accomplishments. They tend to make unpolished statements based on egoism. They immerse themselves in self-satisfaction. They not only fail to contribute anything to society, but as human beings their attitudes are underdeveloped and their actions are childish. What is important about Reigisaho is that it is not simply a matter of bowing properly. The basis of Reigisaho is the accomplishment of the purified inner self and the personal dignity essential to the martial artist.

If we advance this way of thinking, the matter of Reigisaho becomes the question of how one should live life itself. It determines what one's mental frame and physical posture should be prior to any conflict situation. Furthermore, in the actual conflict situation, the guard-posture must have no openings. Thus, Reigisaho originates in a sincere and serious confrontation with life and death. Above all, Reigisaho is an expression of mutual respect in person-to-person encounters, a respect for each other's personalities, a respect which results from the martial artist's confrontations with life-or-death situations.

The culmination of the martial artist's experience is the expression of love for all humanity. This expression of love for all of humanity is Reigisaho.

The belief that each person is important functions as a filter to purify and sublimate the martial artist's personality and dignity. Reigisaho thus melts into a harmonious whole with the personal power and confidence that the martial artist possesses. This coming together establishes a peaceful, secure, and stable inner self which appears externally as the martial artist's personal dignity. Hence, a respectful personality with the strength and independence is actualized. Therefore, Reigisaho is a form of self-expression. The formalized actions of Reigisaho reveal the total knowledge and personality of the martial artist.

We, who are trying to actualize ourselves through Aikido, should recognize that we are each independent. Only with such deep awareness of the self can we carry out a highly polished Rei with confidence.

In short, Reigisaho is to sit and bow perfectly and with dignity. In this formalized expression of Rei, there exists the martial artist's expression of self resulting from his or her philosophy of life and death. For this reason, the martial artist shows merciful care and concern for those who walk on the same path. The martial artists show merciful care and concern for all who seek to develop themselves in mind, body and spirit, with sincere respect for other human lives.

In order for any external, physical act to be complete, it must be an expression of the total person. Abstractly, the external form includes the inside. This is a complete form. For Reigisaho, that means that the external act was from the deep heart or mind. Also, the heart or mind was using the external act for its expression. This is a complete act. The formalized expression of the inner and outer person harmonized in the Saho of the Reigi.

Saho (Formalized Expression of Rei)

Reigisaho thus contains varied implications regarding the inner life, but the observable form is a straightforward expression of respect for others, eliminating all unnecessary motions and leaving no trace of inattention. In the handling of martial art weapons, the safest and most rational procedure has been formalized so that injury will not fall upon others as well as on oneself. Ultimately, the formalized movements become a natural movement of the martial artist who has become one with the particular weapon. Below is an outline of the basics of Saho which I consider necessary knowledge for the martial artist.

1. Seiza (Formal Japanese-Style Sitting)

From your natural standing position, draw your left leg slightly backwards (in some cases the right leg), kneel down on your left knee while staying on your toes. Then kneel on your right knee, lining up both feet while on your toes. Sit down slowly on both heels, as you straighten your toes, placing them flat on the floor so that you sit on the soles of your feet. Place either your left big toe on your right big toe, or have both big toes lightly touch each other side by side.

Next, place both hands on your thighs with fingers pointing slightly inward. Spread out both elbows very slightly but naturally, dropping the tension in your shoulders into the tanden or the pit of the stomach. Raise your sternum which will naturally straighten your back (do not stiffen your back), the knees on the floor should be about the width of two or three fists.

2. Rei before the Kamiza (Front Altar)

From the seiza position, slide both palms of your hands forward to the floor about a foot in front of you, forming a triangle, and then bow by lowering your face slowly and quietly towards the center of the triangle. Do not raise your hip or round your back as you do so; it is important to bend your body at the waist, keeping the back straight as possible. After a brief pause, gradually raise your bowed head pulling up both hands at the same time. Return both hands to the original seiza position and look straight forward.

3. Rei towards fellow students

From the position of seiza, slide your left hand forward slowly, followed by the right hand, and place them on the floor about a foot in front of you and form a triangle, identical to the procedures described above. Following the bow, pull back your right hand while raising your body, followed by the left hand, and return to the original seiza position.

4. Rei towards teachers

The same etiquette as above is observed for bowing to your teacher, but the student should remember to lower his or her head in a bow before the teacher does, and to raise his or her own head after the teacher raises his or hers. Please remember that your bow shows your mental readiness.

5. Standing from the seiza position

First get on your toes, then begin to stand as you move your right foot (or left foot) half a step forward. Stand up slowly and quietly and pull back the right foot (or left foot) so that you are standing naturally.

6. Saho when holding sword (and other weapons)

The sword is normally placed on the sword stand with the handle to the left of you and the blade facing upward (the side of the sword thus seen is called the front of the sword). The placement of the sword is reserved for self-protection in cases of emergencies and when retiring at night.

(a) Rei to the sword (standing)

Take the sword from the sword stand with your right hand grasping the scabbard near the sword guard with the right thumb pressing the sword guard. Then turn up your right hand, placing the handle to your right. Open your right palm holding the sword with the blade turned upwards, while at the same time the thumb of the left hand, palm down holds the scabbard closer to the tip. The sword should be held up at eye level and the bow should be made slowly from the waist with the back kept straight. The sword is raised slightly during the bow.

(b) Rei to the Kamiza (standing)

From the standing bow to the sword, lower the sword in front of you, thus bringing it closer to your body. With your right hand, turn the handle upward with the blade facing you. The sword is held vertically with the right hand in front of your center, and the left hand now grasps the scabbard immediately below the right hand. The right hand then is freed, permitting it to grasp the backside of the sword blade from above. The right hand thus grasping the scabbard should have its index finger placed on the backside pointing towards the sword's tip. Hold the sword close to the right side of your body with the tip turned towards the front at a 35 degree angle and with your right hand at your hip bone. Stand erectly and piously make your bow to the Kamiza. The bow should be about 45 degrees, and you should pull your chin in while you bow.

(c) Rei in front of Kamiza (sitting)

Sit in seiza. Place the sword on the floor on the right side of your body with the blade pointing towards you. The sword should be parallel to your body. Slide both hands simultaneously down from your thighs to the floor and bow to the Kamiza.

(d) Rei towards fellow students and teachers (sitting)

The same procedure should be followed as in the case above, except for the different sequences of putting down your left hand on the floor first when bowing and pulling up your right hand first when rising from the bowing position.

This concludes the description of the minimally required basics of Reigisaho. The brevity of the explanations was intended to avoid possible confusion, but may also have led to lack of clarity and thoroughness of explanation concerning certain procedures. If I have not been generous enough in writing my description of Reigisaho, then I hope that you will forgive me and give to me and others the chance to teach you more in the future.

Shihan Mitsugi Saotome

Philosophy of Aikido

The basic techniques of Aikido derive from the classical Japanese martial arts. The *bujutsu,* the arts of the sword, the spear, and empty hand combat, were developed on the battlefield during hundreds of years of Japanese civil war, systematically created and refined from the reality of life and death situations. During the *Edo* period, the classical bujutsu were studied as a form of self-defense among the elite samurai society for the conflicts had moved from the battlefield into the castles and homes. Evolving from the life style of the samurai, *suwari waza, hanmi handachi, iaido,* all speak of fighting within the confines of castle walls rather than on an open field of battle.

Saotome Sensei is Chief Instructor of the Washington, D.C. Aikikai. He also heads the organization known as Aikido Schools of Ueshiba. Saotome Sensei was a personal student of O'Sensei for many years. This article "Principals of Aikido" was written by Saotome Sensei expressly for this book.

This evolution is obvious in the techniques of Aikido. The Founder of Aikido, Morihei Ueshiba, studied the many arts of bujutsu from the greatest masters of his time, *Daito ryu jujutsu* under Sogaku Takeda, many other styles of jujutsu, many styles of sword and spear, even more modern combat such as bayonet training. Yet O'Sensei was also a deeply spiritual man and studied all manner of traditional spiritual thought.

Throughout his life of asceticism, O'Sensei ceaselessly sought to unite his spiritual beliefs with his mastery of the arts of war. After a time of severe training, he experienced the golden light of enlightenment. The character in bujutsu and in budo literally means to stop the thrusting spear. In his enlightenment, O'Sensei realized that the purpose of budo is to protect all of life, all of society. We are all a part of the same universal energy, the same life force. The enemy is not just your brother, the enemy is a part of yourself. The realization that the universe is in all being is the mission of budo. It is this spirit and realization which sets Aikido apart from the classical bujutsu.

In your practice of Aikido, as well as in your life, you must become consciously aware of and touch with your spirit, the universal life force. In the Orient, this force containing elements of physical and spiritual power is known as *Ki*. This energy, which cannot be stopped but is constantly moving, is manifested through Aikido technique. The power of Aikido recreates the image of the universe which already lives within our body and spirit. The movement of Aikido led the movement of the solar system, the double spiral of the DNA molecule, the power of the nucleus of an atom. It is the movement of life.

O'Sensei taught that this movement is the power of fire and water, the movements of the universal life force. The principles

Shihan Mitsugi Saotome

of *yin* (centrifugal power) and *yang* (centripetal power), the expansion and contraction in nature are manifested in the techniques of Aikido creating harmony of mind and spirit. This spiritual and physical energy must unite to produce the power of Ki to function in the execution of technique.

You must listen to your instincts, the natural feedback system of your mind and body, to react spontaneously. You must learn to trust your intuition. You must awaken the eighth sense, that sense which opens the door to the universal realization, so you can understand the workings of the universe within your own life; so that you can attain the true freedom and independence of this realization. And, for a moment, you will know that your life is not limited, but forever.

O'Sensei said, "When you have an opponent with a mind of conflict and hatred, thinking enemy, you are not free. You cannot be open to the secret of Aikido. True Budo is to harmonize with this world and establish peace." In order to fulfill your mission given by the universal creative consciousness it is important that your mind be free of selfish ego, greed and deceit. Only in this way can you be truly free and one with the power of the universe within your body and spirit.

To save our world in this time of crisis, it is imperative that each one of us purifies our spirit and awakens to the same universal life force which is within us all. We are a part of the universe and a part of each other, not separate. Each of us must release our potential through the strength of self-confidence, love of all life and the spirit of protection for all beings if we are to continue to survive on this planet. This is the secret of Aikido.

Excercises

Jumbi taiso are traditional exercises specifically designed to prepare the body for training. They are an important part of the Aikido experience.

The following exercises are examples. Try to use them as a guide in conjunction with what you have been shown in class. There are many more that have other meanings and functions behind them.

Arm Rotations

1. Forward and backward (both arms together).

2. One forward and one backward (concurrently).

3. Upward arm swing while stretching your wrists (alternate the front hand).

4. Side to side arm swing (hand blade extending outward).

5. Side to side stretch (hands clasped with elbows at shoulder level).

6. Stretch to heavens, then to earth (arms crossed in front).

7. Overhead side stretch (reach overhead from left to right).

8. Full circle body rotation (arms crossed, stretch to heaven and earth).

Leg Stretching (Standing)

9. Spread feet shoulder width, hands on knees, squat down.

10. Spread feet, half squat, hands on knees, lock elbows, twist left and then right. Do these slowly.

11. Keep feet spread and flat on the mat, lower body down with one leg extended, face forward, stretch leg. (Repeat on both sides and then repeat again with the toe of the extended leg pointing straight up. It is important to keep both heels on the mat).

12. Feet wide apart, grasp ankles, legs straight, stretch head down.

Knee Stretch (Standing)

13. Feet together, hands on knees, legs straight, stretch knees back.

14. Knees together, hands on knees, stretch towards left and then to the right.

15. Knees together, hands on knees, rotate knees to the left and then to the right, making a complete circle each time.

16. Knees together, hands on knees, squat deeply keeping heels on the mat.

Leg Stretching (Sitting)

17. Sit down, legs straight, extended out in front of you. Stretch by reaching out over toes (point toes up and back towards head).

18. Spread feet as wide as possible, stretch to the left and then to the right by lowering the chest down to the knee.

19. Repeat #18, reaching with the right hand to the left foot and then with the left hand to the right foot.

20. Adjust your feet to widest possible position, reach out trying to touch your chest to the mat in front (keep your chin up and back straight).

21. Legs still spread, twist at the waist, look behind, reach back placing one hand on the mat and lowering face to the mat (repeat on the opposite side).

22. Feet together, grasp ankles and stretch so that chest touches knees (keep your chin up and back straight).

Ankle Stretch (Sitting)

23. Grasp right ankle with right hand, pull foot up and over left thigh with both hands, stretch (be careful, not too hard).

24. Hold ankle stationary with right hand, rotate foot and ankle with other hand holding the large toe only (first in a forward rotation and then in a backward rotation).

25. Hold foot with right hand near your instep, grasp toes with left hand and then rotate, first forward and then backward.

26. Same position as in #25, stretch toes forward and then backward.

27. With both thumbs, massage toes and then proceed down the entire bottom of the foot.

28. Loosen muscles in the bottom of the foot by striking with the flat side of the fist gently, then with both hand blades.

29. Holding ankle with right hand, and heel with left hand, shake foot until it feels real loose and free of all tension.

30. Grasp ball of foot with right hand and stretch out leg towards front and set leg and foot down.

31-38 Repeat exercises 23-30 on the left ankle.

39. Feet together, repeat #22 and stretch over toes.

40. Grasp both ankles with both hands and pull legs in so that the bottoms of feet contact each other, hold feet together by grasping toes of both feet with both hands, stretch so that chest touches feet.

41. Pull feet up under you and sit seiza. Readjust your gi.

Stretches in Seiza Position

42. Loosen up muscles by striking your body with the flat side of fist gently; start at inner thigh, tops of thighs, outside of legs, buttocks, lower back, in front to the chest, shoulder, down the arm and then under the arm pit. Repeat on the right side with the left hand. End with both hands to the chest.

43. Reach with both hands to the heavens while inhaling through the nose, compress breath into your abdomen, exhale and begin to strike the back of the neck gently.

44. With fingertips of both hands, massage neck (first the back of the neck and then both sides).

45. Stretch neck by letting head drop straight back, return to upright and then back again (repeat five times).

46. Stretch neck as in #45 to the front, left side, and right side (as if trying to touch your ear to your shoulder, making sure to keep your posture upright), looking left, and looking right. Relaxing the neck, let your head swing through a circle, first to the left and then to the right.

47. Relaxing arms, rotate shoulders forward then backwards.

48. Full forward arm rotation reaching outward all the way (twice), then reversing, reach out and inhale through the nose while reaching up to the heavens and spreading hands wide apart, compress breath by bringing hands in to shoulders, and exhale slowly through the mouth while dropping hands down slowly to match the breath (repeat three times).

49. Twist at the waist to the left and then to the right while relaxing the arms and maintaining good seiza position.

Wrist stretches (can be done standing if your legs hurt).

50. Nikkyo (palm down)

51. Kote Gaeshi

52. Nikkyo (thumb pointed down)

53. Sankyo

54. Stretch fingers by grasping the right fingers with the left hand and stretching outward and down, keeping the palm facing away from you (repeat 10 times).

55. Relaxing hands, shake vigorously overhead, then once more down with hands dangling at either side.

56. If you have maintained seiza while doing the wrist stretches, assume a squat position up on your toes with knees wide apart and heels together. Your posture should be good. Hold this position while maintaining your balance.

57. Come to a standing position and stretch legs by doing a few deep knee bends slowly, keeping knees together. Slowly assume an upright standing posture.

Vocabulary and Terminology

This appendix consists of six parts: **Basic Terminology, Common Dojo Phrases, Words of Attack, Parts of the Body, Counting to Ten, and Terms that have Greater Meanings**. By studying the definitions, you will discover many different facets of Aikido philosophy. It is important to your practice of Aikido that you have a basic understanding of these words and be able to use them in practice. Quotation marks indicate the words of the Founder. The Japanese word or term is in bold, followed by the phonetic spelling in parentheses and then the basic definition.

(Note: The definition given may not be the only way to define a word or term; especially since some Japanese terms cannot be translated literally into the English language.)

Basic Terminology

Japanese word or term (Phonetic Spelling) -- Definition

Ai (eye) -- Harmony, unity to join or become one with. The word carries the feeling of the strength and power of natural forces.

Ki (key) -- Spirit; life force or vital energy; the essence of universal creative energy.

Do (doe) -- The Way or Path. "The Way" means to be one with the will of the Universe and embody its function. If you are even slightly apart from it, it is no longer the "Way."

Atemi Waza (ah-teh-mee-wah-zah) -- Striking techniques, blows.

Bokken (bow-ken) -- Wooden sword used in practice.

Budo (boo-doe) -- Literally, the Way of the Warrior arts; but the deeper meaning is the Way of the protection of society, of strength and honor in peace. "A mind to serve for the peace of all human beings in the world is needed in Aikido, and not the mind of one who wishes to be strong and practices only to fell an opponent. There are neither opponents nor enemies for true budo. Therefore, to compete in techniques, winning and losing, it is not true budo. True budo knows no defeat. 'Never defeated' means never fighting."

Bushido (boo-she-doe) -- Warrior's Code, "Way of the Warrior."

Dan (dawn) -- Aikido rank, grade holder, black belt rank.

Deshi (deh-she) -- Student, pupil, disciple.

Dojo (doe-joe) -- The place where the Way is revealed. A place for strengthening and refinement of body, mind, and spirit.

(Formerly, a term used by Buddhist priests in reference to the place of worship.)

Dojo cho (doe-joe choe) -- Term used for the head of the dojo; dojo leader.

Doshu (doe-shoo) -- Honorary title for the Master of the Art. Present Doshu is Kisshomaru Ueshiba, son of the late O'Sensei, Morihei Ueshiba.

Fuku Shidoin (foo-koo she-doe-een) -- Title used for assistant instructor; usually second Dan and below.

Gaeshi (guy-she) -- To reverse.

Gi (ghee) -- White training uniform.

Hakama (ha-kah-mah) -- White-skirted pants worn over the gi. Symbol of the Samurai culture and an important part of the Aikido training uniform. Typically worn by yudansha.

Hanmi (hawn-mee) -- The relaxed triangular stance of Aikido, stable yet flexible enough to move quickly in any direction.

Hanmi Handachi (hawn-mee hawn-dah-chee) -- Nage is kneeling and opponent attacks from a standing position.

Hantai (hawn-tie) -- In reverse order.

Hara (hah-rah) -- The lower abdomen; the center of life energy, physical and spiritual. Often used as a synonym for "guts", courage.

Hidari (hee-dah-ree) -- Left (direction).

Irimi (ee-ree-mee) -- Moving into and through the line of attack with no thought of escape. Technique of entering and choosing death.

Jo (joe) -- Wooden training staff about 50" long and 3/4" - 1" thick.

Joseki (joe-seh-key) -- Upper side of the mat, opposite the shimoseki.

Jumbi taiso (jume-bee tie-sew) -- Aikido exercises.

Kaiten (kah-ee-ten) -- To revolve or rotate.

Kamae (kah-mye) -- A posture or stance of readiness. There are many different stances, and within each stance there are different positions for the hands or weapon: Jodan-High position, Chudan-Middle position, Gedan-Lower position.

Kamiza (kah-mee-zah) -- Upper seat of the mat, opposite the shimoza.

Kannagara (Kah-nah-gah-rah) -- The stream of God. The flow of creative energy which reaches from the past into the future.

Kata (kah-tah) -- Shoulder

Katana (kah-tah-nah) -- Japanese sword; blade.

Keiko (kay-koe) -- Study or practice. The deeper meaning is reflection and refinement; to return to the original and discover reality. Only through the study of the past, and an appreciation for its experience can we understand the present and refine our spirit.

Ken (Kehn) -- Japanese sword

Kenkyo (kehn-kyo) -- Confidence with modesty.

Kiai (key-eye) -- The release of spiritual and physical power in the form of a piercing scream originating in the hara. Literally a meeting of the spirits.

Kohai (koe-high) -- Junior student. Anyone who begins the study of Aikido. You owe them your help and support.

Kokyu (koe-kyoo) -- Power of breath and life force; the coordination of ki flow and breathing.

Kotodama (koe-toe-dah-mah) -- The spiritual function of sound. Every one-syllable sound has its own spiritual vibration.

Kyu (kyoo) -- White belt grade; a mudansha or undergraduate.

Maai (mah-eye) -- The distance of time and space between uke and nage; the movement of mind, the stream of spirit and the direction in which mind and spirit move, along with physical distance determines the balance and proper use of space.

Migi (mee-ghee) -- Right (direction)

Misogi (mee-sew-ghee) -- Purification of mind, body and spirit. Sweating is misogi; cleaning is misogi; fasting is misogi; keiko is misogi.

Mushin (moo-sheen) -- No mind; a mind without ego. A mind like a mirror which reflects and does not judge.

Musubi (moo-soo-bee) -- Opposites are but different images of the same reality. Musubi is the process of their unification. It is the movement of the spiral.

Nage (nah-gay) -- To throw; the person who throws.

Nai kan gyu (neye kawn gyoe) -- Silence and action; training which teaches us to still the mind and see inside.

Obi (oh-bee) -- Belt (part of the gi).

Omoiyari (oh-moy-yah-ree) -- A mind of concern for others' feeling, safety and situation.

Omote (oh-moe-tay) -- To the front.

O'Sensei (oh-sen-say) -- Great Teacher -- The title used for the Founder of Aikido.

Randori (rawn-doe-ree) -- Freestyle against multiple attack.

Rei (ray) -- To bow; salutation.

Reigi (ray-ghee) -- Rei also translates as Holy Spirit; Gi as manifestation. Combines, it means proper etiquette, to respect the creative force and spirit which is the same in all of us. In essence -- we are different, but one in origin; our bodies are different, but our spirits are the same; our functions are different, yet we share the same responsibility to God.

Ryote (ree-oh-tay) -- Both hands.

Samurai (sah-moo-rye) -- Originally came from the verb "to serve." Noble and honorable, one who has the duty and responsibility of protecting society.

Sempai (sehm-pie) -- Senior student. Anyone who began the study of Aikido before you. You should respect this person's experience.

Seiza (say-zah) -- Formal sitting position, the only proper way to sit on the mat.

Senshin (sen-sheen) -- A purified and cleansed heart and spirit; enlightened attitude.

Sensei (sen-say) -- Teacher; one who gives guidance along the way. Literally means "born before."

Shidoin (she-doe-een) -- Title for Aikido teacher with typically the rank of third Dan.

Shihan (she-hawn) -- Title for a master teacher who has been ranked at least to the grade of sixth Dan.

Shimoseki (she-moe-seh-key) -- The lower side of the mat, opposite the joseki.

Shimoza (shee-moe-zah) -- The lower seat on the mat, opposite the Kamiza.

Shinai (she-nye) -- A split bamboo practice sword.

Shomen (show-men) -- The upper seat, the shrine which houses the picture of the Founder and the spirit of Aikido. Not a religious symbol, but a spiritual one.

Shugyu (shoo-gyoe) -- The day-to-day struggle; the work of education to refine and purify the quality of life.

Suburi (soo-boo-ree) -- Training. Suburi is training as opposed to kumi tachi, which is study (keiko).

Suwari waza (soo-wah-ree wah-zah) -- Techniques beginning with both attacker and defender in formal sitting position, executed from the knees.

Tachi (tah-chee) -- Japanese long sword; can also mean "from the standing position."

Taijutsu (tie-joot-soo) -- Empty-handed techniques.

Takemusu Aiki (tah-keh-moo-soo eye-key) -- Enlightened Aikido. "Aiki has a form, and does not have a form. Aiki is a life which has a form and still flows with change; it expresses itself by changing itself. A form without a form is a word and a poem that expresses the universe limitlessly."

Tanden (tawn-den) -- The center; your center of being.

Tanren (tawn-ren) -- Striking practice with sword or bokken. The same cut is practiced over and over again. This can also be done with a Jo.

Tanto (tawn-toe) -- Wooden practice knife.

Tenkan (ten-kawn) -- Turning to dissipate force.

Uchi deshi (oo-chee deh-she) -- Live-in student; personal student or disciple.

Uke (oo-kay) -- One who receives; the person being thrown.

Ukemi (oo-keh-mee) -- Techniques of falling. The art of protecting oneself from injury. The first and most important step to developing good Aikido technique is learning to take ukemi well.

Ura (oo-rah) -- To the rear.

Waza (wah-zah) -- Technique. Way of . . .

Yudansha (yoo-dawn-shah) -- Black belt rank holders.

Zanshin (zahn-sheen) -- Continuity; remaining aware and prepared for the next attack.

Common Dojo Phrases

Abunai! (ah-boo-nye) -- Watch out! Be careful.

Arigato gozaimasita (ah-ree-gah-toe go-zye-mahsh-tah) -- Thank you for what you did (spoken at the end of practice).

Do itasimasite (doe ee-tahsh-ee-mahsh-teh) -- You're welcome; don't mention it.

Dozo (doe-zoe) -- Please; as in go ahead (this may be an instruction from your teacher when he wants you to begin practice after demonstrating a technique).

Gomen nasai (goe-mehn nah-sigh) -- I'm sorry; forgive me.

Hai yame! (hi yah-meh) -- Please stop! (This will be said by your instructor during keiko when he wants you to stop)

Hajime! (hah-jee-meh) -- Please start! (This will be said by your teacher when he wants you to begin; often said with emphasis.)

Konban wa (cone-bahn wah) -- Good evening.

Konnichi wa (cone-ee-chee wah) -- Good afternoon.

Mokuso! (moke-sew) -- Please come to attention; make yourself ready for keiko; meditate! (This will be said in the form of a command by your Sensei or Sempai at the beginning of class and at the end of class just before the ceremonial opening and closing bow respectively.)

Ogenki desuka? (oh-gehn-key dehs-kah) -- How are you?

Ohayo gazaimasu (oh-high-oh goe-zyemahs) -- Good Morning.

Onegaisimasu (oh-neh-guy-she-mahs) -- Thank you for what we are about to do (spoken at the beginning of practice).

Oyasumi nasai (oh-yah-soo-mee nah-sigh) -- Good night (as in leaving).

Sayanara (sigh-oh-nah-rah) -- Good bye.

121

Words of Attack

Hanmi Handachi (hawn-mee hawn-dah-chee) -- Uke standing, nage sitting.

Jo tori (joe toe-ree) -- Jo taking techniques.

Kao tsuki (cow tsoo-key) -- Punch to the face.

Katate tori (kah-tah-teh toe-ree) -- One hand grab to wrist.

Kata tori (kah-tah toe-ree) -- One hand grab to shoulder.

Kete tsuki (keh-teh tsoo-key) -- Kick to the gut.

Morote tori (moe-row-teh toe-ree) -- Two hands on one.

Mune tori (moo-neh toe-ree) -- One lapel grab from the front.

Mune tsuki (moo-neh tsoo-key) -- Thrust or punch to the gut.

Ryokata tori (ree-oh-kah-tah toe-ree) -- Front two shoulder grab.

Ryote tori (ree-oh-teh toe-ree) -- Both wrists grabbed from the front.

Shomen uchi (show-mehn oo-chee) -- Strike to forehead.

Suwari waza (soo-wah-ree wah-zah) -- Techniques from sitting.

Tachi tori (tah-chee toe-ree) -- Sword taking techniques.

Tanto tori (tawn-toe toe-ree) -- Knife taking techniques.

Ushiro kubishime (oo-she-roe koo-bee-she-meh) -- Back choke.

Ushiro ryokata tori (oo-she-roe ree-oh-kah-tah toe-ree) -- Shoulders grabbed from behind.

Ushiro tekubi tori (oo-she-roe teh-koo-bee toe-ree) -- Both wrists grabbed from behind.

Yoko menuchi (yo-koe meh-new-chee) -- Strike to the side of the head.

Parts of the Body

Ashi (ah-she) -- Foot

Hara (hah-rah) -- Stomach

Hiji (hee-jee) -- Elbow

Hiza (hee-zah) -- Knee

Kata (kah-tah) -- Shoulder

Koshi (koe-she) -- Hip

Kubi (koo-bee) -- Neck

Kuchi (koo-chee) -- Mouth

Me (meh) -- Eye

Men (mehn) -- Head

Mune (moo-neh) -- Chest

Rokkutsu (roe-koot-soo) -- Rib

Senaka (seh-nah-kah) -- Back

Te (teh) -- Hand

Tekubi (teh-koo-bee) -- Wrist

Yubi (you-bee) -- Fingers

Counting to Ten

Ichi (ee-chee) -- One

Ni (knee) -- Two

San (sahn) -- Three

Shi (she) -- Four

Go (goe) -- Five

Roku (row-koo) - six

Siti (she-chee) -- Seven

Hati (hah-chee) -- Eight

Ku (koo) - Nine

Ju (joo) -- Ten

Terms That Have Greater Meanings

Ama no torihune (ah-mah no toe-ree-foo-neh) -- This term is given to an exercise that resembles rowing a boat in a hanmi position. There is reason to devote a whole chapter to this exercise, however, it would end up being so voluminous that one would think the book was on just this topic. It will suffice to say that this exercise is of Shinto origin, to cleanse the mind and spirit. It literally means, "bird boat of heaven." In other words, when you perform this exercise, you row your boat through the spiritual levels of heaven towards purification, as in misogi.

Ama no furitama (ah-mah no foo-ree-tah-mah) -- This term is given to an exercise generally done in combination with the above, Ama no torihune. The hands come together in front of your body, while standing squarely, not in a hanmi. The left hand resting on the upturned palm of the right hand. Arms are extended downward, so that both hands are in front of your hara and then both hands are gently shaken so to relieve all tension in your body. This exercise will immediately follow Ama no torihune each time it is performed. This exercise is also of Shinto origin and once again, there are literally volumes of material written about this exercise.

Hanmi and Ma-Ai (hawn-mee and mah-eye) -- Hanmi and Ma-ai are grouped together because they are both about relationships and both begin to bring your individual movement together with that of your partner. Hanmi is the stance you use for ease of movement, readiness, flexibility, and balance. Ma-ai is the positioning you take to properly practice a technique in order to move through it correctly and finish in exact distance. Hanmi begins by placing one foot in front of the other, a comfortable distance apart. The rear foot is turned slightly outward and the forward foot is straight ahead. The weight is evenly distributed and it is easy to turn around or step in any direction. Your balance is now symbolized by the triangular stance of your feet and the sphere of available movement within which you can turn. Hanmi is used in all Aikido techniques unless otherwise stated. When Hanmi is mutual, such as both people standing with right feet forward, it is called "Ai hanmi." When the stance is mutually opposite, one with left foot forward, and the other with right foot forward, the hanmi is called "Gyaku hanmi." It is necessary in training that both the nage and the uke keep proper hanmi when beginning and finishing a technique.

Ma-ai is essential to understanding Aikido techniques. You begin to develop a keen sense of the area around your body that allows you safety or when you are open to attack. Usually the mai-ai is controlled by the nage, but both persons are responsible for a sensitivity to distance. A uke must understand positioning in order to continue to make a flowing practice. Ma-ai is something that requires your sixth sense in order to participate subtly with your body movement. Try always to remember to practice Ma-ai and Hanmi.

Hara (hah-rah) -- Your Hara is specifically the area of the lower abdomen. It is referred to in Japanese martial arts as the motivation for all movement. Without hara-movement, you will be off-balance and without any power. To develop Hara is also to develop "guts." It is the meeting place for the power of the earth and the power of the heavens. It is the center of the body. We begin to learn about extension by beginning with the Hara. Hara is the base from which your energy extends outward. Your Ki is generated from the Hara. The Hara is only the beginning of understanding power, balance and extension of Ki. When you begin to train in Aikido, your Hara will feel like a bouncing ball, moving from your navel up to your shoulder, back down to your waist, up to your neck and so on. It is as difficult to embody as it is to explain. That is why you have your obi (belt) tied where it is. It is to constantly remind you to drop your weight down and concentrate your movement from the hips and legs and not from those grabbing, strong arms. When you do feel that your Hara is relaxed and steady, around the lower abdomen, then you begin to expand it to become your whole body. So Hara is not just a spot that sits behind your belt knot. It is a concept of channeling your Ki and motivation of movement.

Irimi and **Tenkan** (ee-ree-mee and ten-kawn) -- In Aikido, we have within the movements of all techniques the ancient concept of yin and yang. Tenkan is the motion of turning, or yin, and irimi is the motion entering, or yang. If you look carefully, you will see the nage doing either one or the other or a combination. These are the only two motions we do as nage. The level of your understanding of these motions is your level of understanding of Aikido. All tenkans contain irimi and all irimis contain tenkan. You can practice these movements alone. They can help to develop Hara, balance and groundedness.

Keiko (kay-koe) -- Keiko is the Japanese word used for 'training' in a martial or cultural art. It expresses the idea that we can train our spirit as well as our body. We keep the use of this

126

word for our practice to remind us that Aikido is not a sport; it is a study to refine and reflect on the nature of reality and our understanding of it.

Ki (key) -- Ki is the life force that is in us and all around us. It is the consciousness of nature. It is here for us to explore in all aspects of our lives and it is central to understanding Aikido. Ki can mean spirit and energy. It is the life breath. It is the power we will cultivate and define. When we talk about extension, groundedness, Hara (center), kokyu (breath), and other terms, it is all about the way in which we use our Ki. There are no words to explain what Ki is or does. We can tell you how important it is and even ask you to use it. Ki development begins by your trying to find out what it is. You will need to use your imagination and your sensitivity. Then watch and listen to your instructors. Each one will offer you different ideas and approaches to discovering Ki. One thing is certain, however, Ki is the result of your mind, body, and spirit being congruent. It is not physical strength. It is not simply mental desire. It is not just your intuition. It is your skill in combining all of yourself into a common action, into a unified being.

Kokyu and **Musubi** (coe-kyoo and moo-soo-bee) -- Both Kokyu and musubi express the symbology of Aikido's spiralling motions. Kokyu literally means breathing, the power of breath and life force, renewal. The motion in Aikido that symbolizes kokyu is the in and out pulse of the breath. It is the opening of the heart and the extension outward of the life force (ki). It is at the root of all Aikido techniques and its incorporation into your movement is the beginning of understanding O'Sensei's great teaching. It is the symbol of Aikido that teaches us we are all from the same source. Musubi is the blending of kokyu between partners. It is the tying together of Ki. Musubi is the process of unification. Opposites come together and make a whole, a new. Up and down, left and right join together to make a spiral. It is when both people's movement become one. It is the dissolution of conflict. It is the harmony nage teaches to uke. These two concepts are the secrets of Aikido. They are the poetry in the motion and the wisdom of the sage who brought them to us. They teach gentleness and love. We cultivate them graciously.

Misogi (mee-sew-ghee) -- Misogi means purification of mind, body, and spirit. O'Sensei said, "Misogi wa keiko desu." -- training is purification. Sweating is purification. Cleaning is misogi and fasting is misogi. Misogi is the intention of our training and the refining of our skills.

Uke and **Nage** (oo-key and nah-gay) -- The relationship between uke (person taking fall) and nage (person throwing) is one of partnership. There is no competition in Aikido and we change roles easily because we need to be fluent in both halves of each technique. Both are difficult, but the job of the uke seems to be the more complex.

Uke has the task of giving an "honest, sincere, and direct" attack. This means that the extension from your Hara is directed through your body to the Hara or heart-line of your nage. It means that you must give an intelligent attack where your ma-ai, hanmi, and safety are clearly understood. But that's not all. Once the attack is given, you learn to continue your attack until you find you must fall. Eventually your fall is a result of the attack and not a notion you must conclude. Then your skills in ukemi get a turn at the polishing stone. The level of resistance to fall, the over-kill in attack, the holding back in attack, the feat of attack, and fall all mix themselves into the movements. In time, the fine line between continuous attack and artful surrender becomes apparent, yet not all the time. It is the ultimate sensitivity to practice good ukemi. We all are challenged by this role no matter what the level we have attained. It is an open door to a nature and reality that helps Aikidoists transcend their present level. Many people cherish their role as uke as the synthesis of their understanding of the art. Watch carefully the demonstration of both uke and nage. Aikido requires both to work successfully to teach us the harmony of energy.

Nage is responsible for many things as well. When you are a nage it is the time to study the right placement of your movement, to use your kinesthetic sense, and to incorporate the principles and philosophy of Aikido. This is also a challenging job. A key to follow is to try to do the best that you can of what you saw demonstrated, and move in accord with your awareness of the person with whom you are practicing. You should always try to measure your power by the level of the attack from the uke. Of the total energy generated, nage's portion should be at most 30%. Uke's, the other 70%. A good uke is responsive, responsible, and sensitive. A good nage is accurate and skillful.

Zanshin (zahn-sheen) -- Zanshin means calm awareness. It means concern for your partner after the technique is completed and to keep a good martial attitude of alertness. This means watching your partner instead of adjusting your clothes or hair. Be aware of your little habits that separate you from the connection you just developed with your partner. Eye contact, Ki extension, centeredness, all combine to help you develop Zanshin. Without Zanshin, your Aikido becomes sloppy and careless and you could even get hurt. One of the best opportunities to practice Zanshin is on a crowded mat. We never know when a class will be overly crowded or just the right size. People have different schedules and consequently class sizes vary. If you come to class and you notice it is going to be a big one, don't let it discourage you. Adapt your training style. Keep a flexible mind and you will learn to utilize your environment effectively, and you get to truly practice Zanshin. Everything is a reason to train more effectively and to witness the mirror Aikido holds up to you in which you see yourself.